A
VOYAGE OF
MERCY

PETER MCHUGH

A PERSONAL REFLECTION ON PERFORMANCE AND ACCEPTANCE

Unless otherwise stated Scripture taken from the NEW AMERICAN STANDARD BIBLE ®, Copyright © 1960, 1962, 1963, 1968, 1971, 1972, 1975, 1977, 1995 by the Lockman Foundation. Used by permission.

All enquiries regarding this publication and Peter McHugh's speaking engagements should be directed to:

Christian City Church Whitehorse
C3Centre
171 Rooks Road, Vermont, Vic
PO Box 3092, Nunawading BC, Vic 3131

Telephone: 61 3 9837 2900

Email: peter.mchugh@cccw.org.au

Printed and bound by Hyde Park Press, Richmond, South Australia

Book design and cover photography by Philip Hopkins

ISBN 0-9580771-2-6

ENDORSEMENTS

Peter has elucidated in this manuscript issues which I believe are at the heart of Christian discipleship and leadership. They are arguably the most critical issues to be addressed currently within Western Christianity.

Keith Farmer
Former Principal of Australian College of Ministries

At first glance A Voyage of Mercy looks like a wonderful story of God's grace and mercy on the author's life. That in itself makes this a very important book to read. But as I read on I found that Peter McHugh was taking me on a journey that became a personal experience. His brutal honesty disarms the reader from any defences we might normally use to protect ourselves, and makes it easy to swallow the pill of total transformation. May this book be the final nail in the coffin of religion that has brutally restrained the people of God from stepping into our purpose in God. For only in becoming what He has called us to become can we do what He's called us to do.

Bill Johnson
Bethel Church, California, USA

My good friend Peter has captured the essence of God's love for us outside of our performance, in fact, in spite of our performance. Peter's deep thinking, clear insight and reflections on our journey with God reveal the roots that ultimately lead to bearing quality fruit in the Kingdom of God.

Phil Pringle
Founder and President , Christian City Church International

I count it a privilege to consider Peter McHugh as a friend in ministry. He has been a source of inspiration and encouragement to me personally for many years. I admire Peter's openness and authenticity in life and ministry. This book is the result of Peter's deep reflection on his own heart and spiritual journey. The insights he offers have the potential to bring freedom to whoever reads, helping us all to find the fullness of life that is available to us in Christ. I highly recommend it!

Mark Conner
Senior Minister, CityLife Church – Knox, Melbourne, Australia

ENDORSEMENTS

Western culture is performance based, focussing on outcomes and measurable achievements. Western Christianity is not dissimilar. But this book helps us to rediscover that God wants our presence more than our performance. It's who we are, rather than what we do, that helps us to avoid the trap of loving the work of God more than the God of the work.

Dr Stuart Robinson

Senior Pastor, Crossway Baptist Church, Melbourne, Australia

Whether you are a convinced materialist, a wounded and perplexed theist, or just a believer wanting to know the Creator better this book could well be the beginning or the extension of your own Voyage of Mercy. His story moves me to tears and his insights are strength for my soul. Don't miss a word of this powerful and valuable contribution to the journey of faith and life.

Dr. Allan Meyer

Senior Minister, Careforce Church, Melbourne, Australia

I read and then reread Peter's book. Many parts of his journey in ministry have also been mine. Performance. Driveness. Need for Acceptance. Those subjects touched me deeply and opened my self understanding at a new level. I send this word to all my friends: Read the book and let its message do a work in you!

Dale Van Steenis

Founder and Director, Leadership Strategies Incorporated, California, USA

CONTENTS

ACKNOWLEDGMENTS

To the men and women who write and publish books – I am one of the many readers you'll never meet whom you powerfully impact and in whom you leave a legacy.

To Bill Johnson and Graham Cooke – men who have travelled half way around the world to minister in the church I lead and have changed our lives with their message.

To the Executive Leadership Team and staff of Christian City Church Whitehorse – you have created a safe context and loving environment for any who come, but especially for your leader.

To the extraordinary congregation I lead – for your patience and love as I work out my salvation on a voyage of mercy.

To those who walked through my darkest moments with me – you are the true champions of my faith.

To the support crew who have patiently helped me give life to this book – Mick Martin, Briony Scott, Peter Madden, Keith Farmer, Andee Sellman and Fran Sellman, for reading and editing the original manuscript; Rosemarie Searle for her meticulous editing; Lyn McHugh for her invaluable assistance in improving my writing style; Hannah Easton and Erin Sciola for interpreting the scrawl of my handwriting as you typed; Paula Taylor for the typing of the re-written material and assisting Lyn with the tweaking of the writing style; Phil Hopkins for his masterful artwork and layout; and those who contributed your reflections, Wayne Back, Hilary Back, Andee Sellman, Hannah Easton, Paula Taylor, Rick Porter, George Neophytou and Keith Farmer.

ACKNOWLEDGMENTS

To my children and their partners – for helping me be earthed and grounded through your love and unquestioning support.

To my best friend and life companion – Lyn, you are the true believer and I can't thank you enough.

Finally, to my friend Jesus, my greatest support Holy Spirit, and my loving Father God – thankyou.

FOREWORD

Performance is great. We have all witnessed the Olympics where men and women have striven above themselves to win the gold. We have gasped in admiration as athletes after many months of training and conditioning have competed with excellence and distinction.

We love actors and artists, musicians and writers who have all mastered their craft and themselves. The training and discipline involved, not only the finished product, makes us shake our heads in wonder and admiration.

No-one enjoys mediocrity. It is an embarrassment to all concerned. We love talent, especially when it is allied to hard work and diligence. It is a shining example of the human spirit that lifts us all temporarily into a realm of excellence. It captures our imagination and makes us feel something sublime, an extension of who we are in ourselves. It is a privilege to witness that somehow makes the observer more of who they want to be.

There is another type of performance that does the opposite. It is dark, destructive and debilitating. It imprisons people in fear, low self-esteem and a sense of worthlessness. Anytime we do anything in order to feel loved, accepted and valued by others we diminish ourselves all the more.

There are people quick to take advantage of those with such issues. Indeed there are people who deliberately create a climate of non acceptance that enables them to control the performance of others for the corporate good, irrespective of the mental, emotional and physical toll it takes on the individual. Watch the movie *The Devil Wears Prada*. It is a brilliant case study of performance gone wrong, twisted and destructive.

We perform often because we require acceptance or because of our fear of rejection and failure. We are trying to prove something to ourselves or the people around us. It produces a driven attitude that must be continually ramped up until the point of exhaustion and breakdown is reached.

When we apply this type of performance to even simple friendships and relationships around us, they eventually come under enormous strain that produces fracture and collapse. As Christians we can apply this scenario to our relationship with the Father. What you think about God is the most important thing in the world. How you perceive Him and His nature to you will say a great deal about you and how you show up in the earth (Matthew 16:13-20).

Your testimony is not about what you were like before you became a Christian That's your history. Your testimony is about what God is like to you in simple normal relationship. It concerns what you know and have experienced about His character and personality towards you!

When we believe that God is a hard taskmaster, or stern, unapproachable, angry or frustrated, then we cannot be our true selves with Him. We hide our real self away behind our performance. We put up an image that we think God and others want to see.

Instead of accepting God's goodness; revelling in His kindness and mercy and realizing that Jesus is our image and that we are in Him by the design of the Father... we try to earn our place in the Father's heart. We perform because we have not received real love.

Peter has been on a journey out of such a mindset and away from a life that can never know real joy and peace. I have watched Peter's metamorphosis from a nice guy with a business like edge, extreme attention to detail and a sense of drivenness... to a great guy who is relaxed, peaceful, cheerful, much more intimate and friendly. Above all else I have seen his love for the Lord go off the chart. He has become so much more of a worshipper and I believe a man after God's own heart. His faith has increased and his ability to abide in Jesus has changed tremendously. I liked him before... I love him now.

His journey, his story will provide you with insights into the performance condition and valuable keys to move out of your prison into a new level of lovingkindness, acceptance and the best kind of self love.

It's a journey into freedom that all people everywhere should make.

Graham Cooke

Author and Speaker

PROLOGUE

When I remember the early years of our Christian journey together, I easily revisit the sense of excitement, wonder, and awe that we experienced in all that God was doing in our lives. This whole new realm of the Kingdom of God had been opened to us. Possibilities were limitless, risks were there to be taken and there was nothing that our God could not do for us. Even in the pain and the challenge of rebuilding our marriage the goodness of God, His grace and His strength were pre-eminent.

Our learning curves were incredibly steep and the changes we were going through, both internally and in our circumstances, were radical. It was as though we had embarked on a wild ride where the track was now the Word and the will of God, the carriage was His love and His grace, and the force that kept us seated was our faith and trust in Him.

Somehow, subtly, the ride changed. There was less enjoyment and less abandonment to where God was taking us. We were becoming more aware of the drops on either side of the track and the desire to control our speed and direction became stronger. While we were still on track and in the carriage, our seating felt much less secure.

Our faith and trust in God was now mixed with trust in our own efforts. This, in turn, increased the need to make the journey safer, which then led to greater pressure on our performance to ensure 'success' and therefore safety.

The main forces that brought about this change were not evident at the time. While we were aware of the pressures of life and of being in ministry, we were not aware of the greater issues in our souls that were pushing us this way. These issues were different for both of us and we now had to embark on fresh new journeys to that place of complete safety that is found only in total trust in and surrender to God.

PROLOGUE

This book is about Peter's journey and the lessons he learned along the way. Peter has never been half hearted about confronting challenges in his world and this journey was no exception. Through the pain and the difficulties he encountered, his resolve to break through the issues of his inner world never wavered. His conviction that God was leading Him to new places of healing, transformation and freedom carried him through the dark times. He has now found these new places. They are still to be fully explored and experienced but already his sense of excitement and anticipation has been rediscovered. There is a new determination to push further into the supernatural realms of God's Kingdom, despite the risks involved. There is an ease and grace in Peter's world that were missing before and he is more secure than ever in his knowledge of God's love and acceptance.

Those of us close to Peter have all benefited from his willingness to go on this *voyage of mercy*. I thank and honour him for his courage and honesty in facing his fears and his inner secret kingdom so that he, and those around him, can be all God has called us to be.

Lyn McHugh
September 2006

Titus 3 : 4 – 7

But when the kindness of God, our Saviour and His love for mankind appeared, He saved us, not on the basis of deeds which we have done in righteousness, but according to His mercy, by the washing of regeneration and renewing by the Holy Spirit, whom He poured out upon us richly through Jesus Christ our Saviour, so that being justified by His grace we would be made heirs according to the hope of eternal life.

New American Standard Bible

1

YOU BEGAN SO WELL

When man takes one step toward God, God takes more steps toward that man than there are sands in the world of time.

THE WORLD OF THE CHARIOTS

In January, 1982 my life was complicated, painful and at a really low ebb. Lyn and I had married on January 6, 1979. During 1981 I had an affair with someone I was working with in Sydney, Australia. Lyn and I had moved to Canberra at the end of 1981 to try to begin our life together again. Unfortunately, I was unable to keep my commitments to Lyn and we separated on our third wedding anniversary.

Lyn went overseas to England to be with her eldest sister for three months and travel Europe. I went to Adelaide, to watch Australia play cricket against the West Indies. I was 25 years old, a qualified social worker with a year's experience, out of work and somewhat directionless. When I arrived in Adelaide I was offered the opportunity to smoke marijuana. I had already drunk too much alcohol in my life. I was fearful of other drugs, and had successfully avoided them until this point. I accepted the offer.

The next morning I was told by a veteran drug user that what I had smoked was the most potent *grass* they had ever used. I was almost pleased to hear this as I had gone on 'a trip' under the influence of this *dope* and it scared me terribly. I encountered some very dark, demonic creatures that were aggressive beyond belief in the way they tormented me. I was scared.

Walking to and from the Adelaide Cricket Ground I started to entertain the thought that there was a spiritual dimension to life. I wondered if there was a God. My religious upbringing assured me there was, but He was harsh, focused on sin and wanted life to be dull and irrelevant.

Before these events while at Sydney University studying social work, I had met a number of Bible reading and believing Christians. Some were dull and boring, others inconsistent in the practice of their faith, bordering on hypocritical. Then there were the *weird* ones who spoke of angels and spiritual realities, yet they were strangely attractive. One of the *weird* Christians was Mark Kelsey. We ended up working together helping some very dysfunctional families. It was in this work environment that the affair started.

Mark made numerous valiant attempts to share his faith with me. I was caustic in my response. I sang the praises of my Marxist philosophy to him in an attempt to win him to my belief systems. Mark finally realised he was not going to make any impact on my rejection of God so stopped telling me about his faith. However, he never stopped

MARK MADE NUMEROUS VALIANT ATTEMPTS TO SHARE HIS FAITH WITH ME.

praying for me, nor did he stop treating me with concern and care. Mark was married to a gentle woman named Bernadette, and together they exuded peace, certainty and a confident love for each other.

While I was in Adelaide having my first encounter with demonic beings under the influence of drugs, the woman I was now courting was staying at Mark and Bernie's in Sydney. She was being influenced by their God talk and wanted me to hear their point of view. Flying back to Sydney, I determined not to be drawn into Mark's desire for me to adopt the Christian Faith. When the suggestion to attend church was finally made however, I agreed to attend. (If only to gather evidence that my perspective of religion being an 'opiate for the masses' was correct.)

Arriving at church was like walking onto the set of a *Blues Brothers* movie. People were clapping, dancing, lifting their hands in the air to music that was fun and more akin to what I was accustomed to as a child of the seventies. It was lively and passionate. Meeting in a converted warehouse, about 150 people were entering into this experience enthusiastically. The sermon was entertaining and fun to listen to, and even made sense. That was the morning service.

There was an evening service at 6pm. After an afternoon of debating the merits of the morning's experience I protested a little at going back, but inwardly was actually looking forward to it. I had some vague and nondescript thoughts beginning to formulate that this church may have something to add to my recent reflections about the possible existence of God.

The evening service was more full-on than the morning. The preacher was Phil Pringle and was he excited! People from the congregation were responding to invitations for prayer and going down to the front of the church. When Phil prayed for them it was louder than I was used to. He laid his hand on their heads. They then fell over and someone caught them before they hit the concrete floor. Now this I had not seen before! Why and how they were falling escaped me but my cynicism was convinced it wasn't real. Yet somewhere deep down inside of me I could accept it. My head was screaming that what I was experiencing was nonsense. My heart was quietly embracing the experience and atmosphere as being warm and comforting.

Phil concluded the service with what was a very entertaining sermon. We were all asked to close our eyes. Now things were going to get really interesting. Phil asked if anyone wanted to become a Christian. He went on to say this was possible by raising a hand in acknowledgement and repeating a simple prayer.

Everything in my intellectual world was crying out to declare this was all rubbish. I had argued with Christians at University and successfully defeated their logic every time. I had even convinced some they were wrong and they abandoned their faith. Yet somewhere from within me came the surging desire to say *yes* to the invitation Phil was offering.

EVERYTHING IN MY INTELLECTUAL WORLD WAS CRYING OUT TO DECLARE THIS WAS ALL RUBBISH.

I recall my right hand going up, looking at it and deliberately pulling it down, only to find my left hand in the air. There was an internal battle being waged between my head saying no and my heart saying yes. I didn't know it then but it is true that your heart can take you places your head will never go.

Those who raised their hands were invited to come to the front of the church to be prayed for. The battle continued with my mind demanding that I stay put while my heart was bursting with anticipation. Somehow I found myself walking towards Phil.

Six of us arrived at the front – including the woman with whom I had had the affair. I can't remember what I prayed but I can recall thinking that Phil was not going to 'push me over' like he had done to others earlier in the evening. When we had prayed out loud asking Jesus to be Lord of our lives, Phil moved along the line, praying for us. I braced myself for this moment when, before Phil laid a hand on me, I found myself falling over and being caught. As I began to fall I started to cry. I cried for a long time. When I stopped, I felt incredibly different. If I had to use language to describe what was really indescribable, I would use words like light, free, clear, clean and open. My voyage of mercy was well underway.

There were times in the past when I had tried to read the Bible. At the age of eight I wanted to become a catholic priest. I even had a neighbour,

Mrs Proudfoot, committed to making my vestments. When I was around 13 or 14 years of age, I recall often picking up the Bible to read, but it made no sense to me. When I discovered girls and my hormones, the idea of being a celibate priest was not so attractive. Teenage parties, sport, alcohol, perceived hypocrisy in church life and teaching, all resulted in the abandonment of my religious life let alone spiritual awareness. Later my debates at university with Mark and others, notably Lyn's sister Karen and her now husband Tim, required some Bible knowledge. However, this was to win arguments, not change my heart.

Following my acceptance of Jesus as Lord of my life that Sunday I began to read the Bible with new application the very next day. It was now making sense. I could feel the words impacting me with peace, warmth, and an overall sense of well being. On the Wednesday, three days after becoming a Christian, I was in Mark and Bernie's home on my own. I was lying on a couch reading the Bible I had bought for myself. I remember putting it down on my chest to reflect on what I had been reading. As I was reflecting I felt a surge of strength enter my body. Then, without warning, my tongue was moving uncontrollably around inside my mouth. It sounded like babble but felt like a language. This activity lasted for about a minute and stopped as abruptly as it had started.

I had enough psychology in my Social Work degree to know this was not normal human behaviour. I was confused and overwhelmed but was unable to feel frightened. Mark returned to the house from surfing. I told him of my experience and he explained from Scripture that I had been baptised in the Holy Spirit and was speaking in tongues. Prior to this occurrence I had never heard of speaking in tongues let alone it being a spiritual gift I would desire.

So much happened, and so fast, it is all a bit of a blur in my memory now. Shortly after this I stopped drinking alcohol. I poured hundreds of dollars worth down the drain. I found myself no longer swearing. My previously explosive temper was non existent and although I still was angry at times, it was without the heat. Somewhere during this time I was water baptised. I was also delivered from demonic power that was leading me into sexual behaviour

> **SO MUCH HAPPENED, AND SO FAST, IT IS ALL A BIT OF A BLUR IN MY MEMORY NOW.**

that was not appropriate now that I was following Jesus. I also found a desire in me to find reconciliation with Lyn.

I wrote to Lyn in England and described what had taken place. Lyn, understandably, did not want to hear anything from me, let alone news that I had a life changing experience. From a human perspective I had been the one who was 'the villain'. I had broken her heart, destroyed our relationship, sent out the loudest of rejection messages and sabotaged any reason for her to trust me. Lyn made it very clear she was not interested in my life and did not wish to have further contact. I prayed and felt led to do two things. First, to write to her again. This was only met with a stronger 'leave me alone' message. Second, to visit Karen and Tim and talk with them about my experience. They, like many others, were astonished at my conversion. A Marxist student political leader, who had ridiculed both Christianity and their faith, was now proclaiming the truth of the life changing work of Jesus in a person's life. I left a gift for Lyn with them as I knew she would stay there on her return from England.

Lyn did indeed stay with Karen and Tim and was told I had been to see them. They said I was a changed person and encouraged her to get in touch. Lyn reluctantly made the phone call. We talked and I asked if I could visit. Lyn's first response was negative, but she later she agreed. We met at Karen and Tim's place. In the conversation that followed I told Lyn all that had happened for me in the past three months. She spoke of God thoughts and spiritual awareness that had happened for her while she was travelling in Europe. After a three hour conversation I boldly asked if she would like to pray as I had. Lyn asked Jesus into her life but was not ready to ask me back.

We went to Phil's church service the next week. This was extraordinarily courageous on Lyn's part. The woman with whom I had had the affair was now actively involved and attending this same church. That Sunday morning Lyn made a public declaration of her faith by responding to the altar call to ask Jesus to be her Lord and Saviour. Over the next four months we lived in separate flats while pursuing a relationship akin to dating. We prayed, read our Bibles, went to small groups and regularly attended church. We then agreed that the Lord was keen for us to rebuild our marriage. Soon after we found out Lyn was pregnant with our first child Hannah. We believed the Lord was asking me to do a one year Bible College course in preparation to enter full time ministry. Paradoxically we also believed the Lord had directed Lyn to stop working as a high-school teacher.

Twelve months after my conversion I had no work; I was attending Bible College 20 hours a week; Lyn was three months pregnant and not working; and, we had resumed living together as husband and wife. We learned so much during this year. Our faith for financial provision was extended and built upon. Our call to ministry grew louder as I worked voluntarily for the church in pastoral activities. Our love for, and trust in one another was beginning to grow. We encountered many challenges but negotiated them together. There were so many miracles of provision and redemption it would take too long to recount.

Suffice to say, after being a Christian for two and a half years I found myself employed on the staff of Phil's rapidly growing church. During the next twelve months we helped as team members in planting a church in Sydney. Then, after three and a half years, we moved to Canberra to start a church as team leaders. This plant went fabulously well and we returned to Sydney after 20 months where I rejoined Phil's staff as Bible College Principal.

WE LOOK BACK ON THESE YEARS AND THINK HOW DID WE DO ALL THAT?

We look back on these years and think how did we do all that? Our second child, Erin, was born six weeks after moving to Canberra and two years after Hannah. Our third child, David, was born three months after we returned to Sydney. We bought our first home in Sydney 12 months later while knowing that somewhere in the future we would plant another church. Little did we realise we would only be in Sydney two and a half years before moving to Melbourne, a place where we knew only one couple, to start the church we lead today.

Clearly, the glory belongs to God for all that took place in those eight years. Yet, the focus of this writing is not on the beginning. The beginning creates the context for what was to occur some 20 years later through 2004 and into 2006. Paul writes in Galatians 3:3, *"Are you so foolish? Having begun by the Spirit, are you now being perfected by the flesh?"*

It is my hope that the account that follows of my voyage of mercy through these years will help others find their way again to an expression of Christianity that is not just life enhancing but rather, life changing.

"You foolish Galatians, who has bewitched you, before whose eyes Jesus Christ was publicly portrayed as crucified? This is the only thing I want to find out from you: did you receive the Spirit by the works of the Law, or by hearing with faith? Are you so foolish? Having begun by the Spirit, are you now being perfected by the flesh? Did you suffer so many things in vain – if indeed it was in vain? So then, does He who provides you with the Spirit and works miracles among you, do it by the works of the Law, or by hearing with faith?" (Galatians 3:1-5)

So Why Write?

To know what you prefer instead of humbly saying amen to what the world tells you you ought to prefer, is to have kept your soul.

ROBERT LOUIS STEVENSON

So Why Write?

It's over 20 years since those early glorious days. Lyn and I planted a church three years after becoming Christians. It grew and was seen to be successful. We moved and planted a second church which grew rapidly in its first six years. Then some significant challenges came along. We negotiated our way through them but it was extremely painful. I lost confidence as a leader and it took a number of years to feel secure again. After I had been leading this fabulous congregation for 16 years I now looked ahead to the next 20 years of following Jesus as a church leader. While reflecting what those years would look like, some burning questions arose inside of me. I thought there had to more spiritually than this. More than I was experiencing. More of God to experience, for those I was leading as well.

My questioning revolved around my motivations for leading. They included how I was leading. What were the internal paradigms I was leading from? The voyage to this point had been at times thrilling, eventful, painful and fruitful. Yet deep down there was a yearning to experience more of God's peace. I wanted a greater measure of *the rest* of faith (Hebrews 4:1-6). I longed for a deep, abiding and personal reality that following Jesus meant things were *light and easy* (Matthew 11:30). Church life had to rise well above administrating programs. I longed to discover who God really could be for me in my daily life. It was now time to see our *normal Christian life* reflect that of the New Testament.

As I pursued answers I was led to unexpected places. Places in my secret inner world. Thoughts, ideas and beliefs that did not conform to God's word, to His view of me, and my view of Him. This was to be a profound part of my voyage of mercy and it has changed me deeply.

Here are comments from those closest to me about the change, its impact and outcomes. These observations are not intended to be self serving nor self congratulatory. Rather they are to illustrate both the process I engaged in, and to encourage others to begin their own journeys. There are redemptive works of God that are only completed in community (James 5:16 ; 2 Corinthians 12:9). The twin ideologies of individualism and consumerism can rob us of the work God does when we are genuinely living in community. Individualism supports a faith that is private. Scripture encourages a faith that is public in gathering together and being sent out (John 17:18,20; Hebrews 10:24-25). Consumerism validates the practice of moving from one church to another. However, when relationships are stretched we can learn what we are contributing to the tension and seek the Helper's aid in being transformed (Matthew 7:1-5; Colossians 3:12-15).

WAYNE BACK (EXECUTIVE PASTOR)

My perception was that the old Peter had a value and a desire to be relational that was in conflict with an inner drivenness that wanted to make sure the tasks were performed in great detail. This meant for me that there were two Peter's – one trying hard to be relational and the other highly focused and detail oriented. There didn't seem to be anything in between and I was never sure which one I would get. Now there is just one Peter. The change has been quite remarkable. I find that Peter is now pretty much the same person in all circumstances whether facing difficulty or doing the mundane things

HIS LEADERSHIP COMES OUT OF WHO HE IS RATHER THAN WHAT HE IS TRYING TO DO.

or having fun. His leadership comes out of who he is rather than what he is trying to do. The new Peter is accepting and relational... I have been amazed at the changes. It has been a testimony to me as to how the very nature of a person can be transformed by the Holy Spirit. Peter obviously had to flow with what God was doing and it was, like all of us, out of a dark time that he allowed the light of God to shine.

Rick Porter and George Neophytou (Members of the Executive Leadership Team)

We have worked with Peter in a joint governance capacity for a number of years and knew him as a task and performance oriented leader. We were not hugely surprised when Peter mentioned to us that God had shown him some things around these characteristics that He wanted him to deal with.

In working quite closely with Peter throughout the ensuing months we observed his journey and believe there were a number underlying keys to a successful conclusion and eventual victory for him. These included our belief that God had put him in his role as Senior Minister, and that the process was necessary for him to achieve his full potential in God.

Andee Sellman (Church Business Leader)

I have always loved and respected Peter's ability to see the big picture strategically and be able to very quickly work out what needed to be done and then go ahead and get it done. The last eighteen months have been about *letting* things happen rather than *making* them happen. As a result it has meant that more input is taken from others and there is the opportunity to allow that input to shape the direction of decisions. I guess it must often be frustrating for Peter to see things much quicker than others and need to allow time for people to catch up...It never ceases to amaze me how he is prepared to make himself vulnerable and accountable to others. I have seen a few senior ministers and never before have I experienced one who so openly makes himself accountable to other people. While I am not aware of any of the detail of the process that George and Rick went through with Peter, it would have not been easy. But through it I believe the Lord found someone who, because they were prepared to be accountable, could be relied on and trusted with great spiritual authority. I believe that often people look to the Lord to do a work without being prepared for the fact that he might use human beings to help in the process. Peter's common sense to set up a process where there was accountability to people, as well as the Lord, meant there was the opportunity for gaining the best 'bang for buck' in the whole situation. I also think that the process of using prayer support as part of the spiritual insight showed great courage and accountability.

PAULA TAYLOR (MY PERSONAL ASSISTANT)

There has never any doubt in my mind that Peter loves the Lord. I have always seen him as a passionate preacher and a supremely competent leader. When I moved from congregational member to staff member I bumped into another Peter. This Peter could be quite formidable! This Peter had a plan for everything, and the plan was not to be tampered with. The phrase I remember him using the most when being told his plans may need adjusting was "That doesn't work for me". I began to realise that meant "Just get it done anyway". I put myself under tremendous pressure to do the stuff, meeting deadlines to keep him pleased with me. They say 'more is caught than taught', and I was learning that performance was paramount.

As Peter came out of his dark time it was as though something was lifting from us all. The first time I heard him say "Let's leave it then" after I explained why something would be very difficult to achieve, I knew I had a new boss! As the culture of an organisation is determined from the top down, we are all benefiting from Peter's revelation. I have always loved Peter, but I like him a lot more now too!

HANNAH EASTON (MY ELDEST DAUGHTER)

In the past year, I have seen my father change radically. One of the biggest ways the change has been demonstrated/lived out in my world has been in our ability to relate just as friends. I know without a doubt that Dad is proud of me just because I am his daughter, and even if I made more mistakes and had more 'failures' than successes, he would still be proud of me. To me, this speaks volumes of the change in him internally, because he now knows and is fully assured of his acceptance *just as he is* in God, and therefore he conveys that to us as children, and to the congregation of our church.

I have always known I am loved by Dad. Now, as well as knowing I am loved, I can share my feelings and thoughts with incredible honesty and randomness, being more relaxed in who I am because he is more relaxed and sure of who he is.

Let's go on a journey together. We'll explore the impact of our response to a performance based culture. We'll look at how this response can produce and feed fear and insecurity in us. We will then examine how this affects the way we live our Christian lives.

The next chapter will explain these ideas in more detail. It will endeavour to focus our thoughts around whether our identities are shaped by performance or acceptance. Our journey will continue as we look at the lessons I learned from passing through some very dark places in my voyage of mercy. The testimony of my time of darkness follows. We will then consider how we may begin to look at our world around the fundamental issues of performance and acceptance.

I feel compelled to write this material, yet nervous. I am very aware of the Lord's call to write. Friends, colleagues and associates have requested that I write both the story of the voyage and its insights. I am nervous about the vulnerability in the personal nature of the testimony that will follow. Yet without it, the lessons I have to share have no context, losing their impact and application. Equally, Scripture calls us to boast about our weaknesses (2 Cor 12:9) and identifies that when I am weak, I am actually strong (2 Cor 12:10). Everything I write is both motivated by and framed within three key assumptions that you should be aware of from the outset.

The first assumption is that the New Testament offers the hope of a normal Christian life that is full of God's power and presence daily (John 15) for every believer. My first 12 months following Jesus was like this. 20 years later I was frustrated and despairing that this was not my reality. I did not see God's power and presence in my congregation and I was not aware of these things being an ongoing reality for other church leaders and their congregations. I was no longer prepared to bring my theology to the level that justified my experience. I needed to search out the things that God had hidden for me (Proverbs 25:2). I wanted to lead out of a faith that was incarnate in me, no longer living as someone

> **I WANTED TO LEAD OUT OF A FAITH THAT WAS INCARNATE IN ME...**

educated way beyond my level of obedience. I longed for a greater awareness of, and appreciation for, the freedom and transformation that were won for me at the Cross.

The second assumption is that increased freedom (Gal 5:1; John 8:31-32) and transformation (2 Cor 3:17-18; Romans 12:2; Titus 2:14) are foundational to God's purpose in our lives. This belief requires a position on the process of change. My belief about the way God changes us is informed by the scriptural truth of sanctification (Romans 6:22; 2 Thessalonians 2:13) as being a journey marked by process and order. The journey begins with salvation (Titus 3:4-7) which is accompanied by experiences ranging from peace through to knowledge, through to radical transformation.

The work of sanctification takes place in the inner secret kingdom of our beliefs, thoughts and ideas. This is the domain of our soul, that is, our mind, emotions and will.

The final assumption is that our inner secret kingdom affects what we see and what we do. Unless a man is born again, he cannot see

WE REPRODUCE AROUND US THE ENVIRONMENT THAT IS WITHIN US.

the kingdom of God (John 3:3). How we see God and His kingdom is directly related to our personal experiences with God and the knowledge we receive from Him (John 3:19-21; 1 John 1:5-6; Ephesians 5:13-14). As a man thinks in his heart so is he (Proverbs 23:7). It is what comes out of us that defines us (Matthew 15:11). We reproduce around us the environment that is within us. We are not to walk in the flesh but in the Spirit (Galatians 5:13-25). Yet it is clear that, like the Galatians (Galatians 3:1-5), we can go from allowing the Holy Spirit to work transformation and freedom into us, to relying on self effort to bring righteousness and peace to our inner secret kingdom.

In addition, most of life and many of the ways of God are understood from the stance of *both/and* more than *either/or*. For example, through Romans 8-10 Paul embraces both predestination and salvation through faith and confession. Many theologians and members of the body of Christ adopt these positions of Scripture as either one or the other. Yet Paul lived with this mystery and paradox from a *both/and* stance. That is, both predestination, and salvation through faith and repentance, are in the heart of God.

These key assumptions are integral to my thoughts and ideas to follow.

I previously summarised the content of this book as: exploring the impact of our response to a performance based culture; how this response has the potential to produce and feed fear and insecurity in us; and the subsequent effect this response has on the way we live our Christian lives.

Fear and insecurity are residents of our inner secret kingdom. They come into existence through the way we interact with the people and circumstances that surround us from the time we are conceived. These people and circumstances are shaped by many forces. One of these influences is the performance base of our culture. Therefore, one of the sources of fear and insecurity in us comes from our response to the expressions of performance we encounter. Our response is influenced by the lies we believe, the hurts we take on board, the wounds we have received through our relationship with others and the circumstances we have lived in.

If fear and insecurity are not changed by our yielding to the process of sanctification, the expectation of Christian life lived out in the New

Testament is limited. That is, a life accompanied by the power and presence of God as evidenced by the fruit of the Spirit and the gifts of the Spirit (signs and wonders with supernatural origins) does not find full expression. The power of fear and insecurity ensures that we return in varying measures to the life of the natural man and its accompanying self effort.

Albert Einstein wrote: The significant problems we face cannot be solved at the same level of thinking that we were at when we first created them. The fears and insecurities created through living according to the demands of a performance based culture cannot be eased by improving our performance. That is, if I pray more, if I pray harder, if I fast, if I read my Bible more, if I tithe, if I do... then God will set me free; He will answer my desire for increase and growth; or He will bless me and all I am pursuing. If I do more, He will do more. This is the basis of the expression of much of Western Christianity.

ALBERT EINSTEIN WROTE: THE SIGNIFICANT PROBLEMS WE FACE CANNOT BE SOLVED AT THE SAME LEVEL OF THINKING THAT WE WERE AT WHEN WE FIRST CREATED THEM.

I have found that the answer to the fear and insecurity I am describing, with its attendant works based, or achievement theology, is found in experiencing the complete acceptance of God. The truth is that God has never been disillusioned with us because He never had any illusions about us in the first place (Romans 5:6-11) God is scandalous in the way He forgives and accepts us (Luke 15:22-24). He looks for every opportunity to celebrate us and rejoice over us.

Then there is a right order for things in God's kingdom. Some things come before others, but not necessarily without them. For example, there is acceptance before performance, but it is not without performance. The Lord wants us to be fruitful (John 15: 8) and engaged in good deeds (1 Tim 6:18-19) – in other words, to perform. However, our performance is neither why we relate to God, nor what we are to be defined by, or the basis of God's blessing. Rather we relate to God from a place of acceptance, assured by His total commitment to us and we receive gifts from Him on the basis of His goodness and holiness. It is from this foundation that we bear fruit (John 15:5), or put another way – we perform. So, we live on the basis of acceptance before performance. Yet, we are not to be self indulgent with the place of our acceptance and ignore the call for the kingdom of heaven to invade earth (Matthew 6:10).

...HOW MUCH OF YOUR IDENTITY IS IN YOUR PERFORMANCE.

The challenge in this book is for you, the reader, to consider the need to examine how much of your identity is tied to your performance. You may be steeped in a performance based mind-set with God and not realize it. I believe there is a voyage of mercy for us all that leads us to extraordinary freedom when we truly know how accepted we are by God. The power and liberty of the Christian life is found in an identity based totally in God's acceptance. Will you allow the words on these pages and the work of the Holy Spirit to launch you into your own voyage of discovery?

SO WHY WRITE?

Lord I pray that those who read this book would be touched by Your mercy. Would you do for them what You have done for me? Would you bring the true freedom of the Gospel to their inner world? Performance no longer sets the agenda. Acceptance by You is the reference point for all they are and do. In Jesus name. Amen.

3

SHOULD,
HAVE TO,
NEED TO,
EXPECTED TO,

To live a creative life, we must lose our fear of being wrong.

JOSEPH CHILTERN PEARCE

SHOULD, HAVE TO, NEED TO, EXPECTED TO

I was raised as the eldest child of a family with two brothers and one sister. We were brought up in a Roman Catholic church. I was an altar boy and went through a very devout stage at the age of eight. My experience within this Christian tradition was strongly influenced by notions of sin, hell, purgatory, confession and rules – lots of rules. God seemed distant, harsh, angry, judgmental and retributive. He was to be pleased through my goodness and appeased by my confession and subsequent praying of multiple 'Hail Mary's' and 'Our Father's'. The knowledge of God was established by rote learning and the Catechism. The emphasis was on getting to heaven and avoiding hell.

My memories of family life are of a 'functioning' family. I recall our life together and the activities we pursued together as being marked by routine. The emotional climate was consistent, being neither warm nor cold. We lived together politely and caringly but never really getting to know one another. I found affirmation when I was good and sought out as many ways as possible to be viewed in this light. I heard that I was loved but was not aware of any sense of well being or security coming from this knowledge. I tried to avoid doing wrong, with varying degrees of success, and always regretted my failures. I was not mistreated or neglected. I was generally unsure of whether my parents were proud of me as I perceived the expectation to always do better.

The experience of school brought a mixed bag of emotions. I was not academic but I was motivated to do well. Anything to do with language – spelling, grammar, learning another language, creative writing – was always painful and negative. I tried hard but never rose above average. I clearly recall the humiliation of regularly coming last in spelling competitions. I cheated at a self assessment English comprehension programme in Year 6 called SRA. My grades were over inflated but no one ever found out. I was more adept at maths and social sciences. I discovered that hard work avoided bad grades and brought the affirmation I was seeking.

At school I discovered both an aptitude for sport and a strongly competitive nature. I was generally nominated as the captain of a team or quickly picked to be on someone else's team. Winning was everything, providing a great sense of well being and value. Whether I was scoring or defending, it was approached with zeal, vigour and incredible determination.

My encounters with the opposite sex from around the age of 15 were marked by feelings of success and failure, acceptance and rejection. Unfortunately, it was more about sexual matters than being friendly and relational. Lessons in control, manipulation and being right were quickly and keenly learned. The 'boys' rewarded this approach again, bringing affirmation, acceptance and value.

Every human being is looking for value and acceptance. We all long for approval and do all we can to avoid rejection. The primary human context of discovering our value, acceptance and approval is the family. However, there is now plenty of evidence to show that most of us grow up in families that are dysfunctional to some extent. For many of us, our families leave us with a gnawing question as to whether we measure up or not.

In the absence of unconditional love, the need for value, acceptance, approval and measuring up are met at some level, on the basis of our performance. Families and cultures have a behavioural standard that those in them are expected to conform to and by which they are judged accordingly. These judgments leave people in little doubt as to their level of approval and acceptance. Consequently, performance becomes a point of defining who we are. We begin to find value and meaning outside of ourselves on the basis of what others expect and how they react.

Failure to meet the behavioural standards and the consequent judgment we receive has to be managed by us all. We begin to establish beliefs about who we are. We begin to fear certain responses, question our adequacy and hence develop insecurities. Our different temperaments and personality styles ensure that we respond to these fears and insecurities in our own way.

Like Don Williams in his book, *Jesus and Addiction*[1], I believe we need to take a fresh look at how the surrounding culture impacts us across our denominational and theological lines. Is it possible that instead of being a prophetic voice to the culture it is in, the church instead mirrors the culture in various ways?

> **IS IT POSSIBLE THAT INSTEAD OF BEING A PROPHETIC VOICE TO THE CULTURE IT IS IN, THE CHURCH INSTEAD MIRRORS THE CULTURE IN VARIOUS WAYS?**

Behavioural standards are rooted in expectations. God clearly has expectations of our behaviour. They are stated in the Old Testament primarily in the Ten Commandments. The standards of the New Testament are extraordinarily high. The expectations of Matthew 5, 6, and 7 are characterized by Jesus' words, *You have heard it said, but I say...* He always said more was expected. In fact, Jesus said, If you love me, you will keep my commandments (John 14:15). What God expects of us behaviourally is extraordinary. Failure is inevitable. Failure on an ongoing basis is the experience of every believer. So, how do we handle our failure?

A Voyage of Mercy

Every church congregation and its denomination or movement has behavioural standards. Each has its own status symbols of acceptance ranging from spiritual experience (water baptism, baptism in the Holy Spirit, experience of salvation), to which Bible translation is used, or whether the consumption of alcohol is acceptable. When new people come to church, they quickly learn the prevailing code of conduct in order to feel welcome. They pursue approval on the basis of conformity. Yet when they fail to conform they are marginalised at best and rejected at worst.

Jesus had similar experiences when He challenged the behavioural standards and beliefs of the prevailing religious community. Firstly, he challenged the accepted basis of salvation and forgiveness. He shifted it away from being centred in the temple, the priesthood and the sacrificial system to being centred in Himself. Secondly, he challenged the accepted basis of community. It was not exclusive but inclusive. Unlike the Pharisees he did not fear being contaminated by sin when mixing with the wrong people. He actually enjoyed their company. God's love was revealed to be inclusive not exclusive. Thirdly, he exploded the sense of piety by declaring it was 'party time'. As Williams says: "it was no longer the law, but the gospel; it was no longer religion, but relationship; it was no longer Moses, but an overwhelming joyful life with Jesus"[2]. Jesus' failure to conform to the behavioural standard resulted in the ultimate rejection of being crucified. He would not allow fear and insecurity to determine His response. Instead He relied on what His Father would do.

The key to living with these behavioural standards is how we deal with the inevitable failure. The message of the book of Hebrews is that God introduced the Ten Commandments to show us that we would fail and we need Him. Jesus said He would send "a Helper" – the Holy Spirit

50

(John 14:16-31; 16:5-15) because He knew we could not possibly meet the expectations and standards He had set forth. Paul in Romans 7, 8 and 9 wrestles with how to respond to failure: *Wretched man that I am! Who will set me free from the body of this death* (Romans 7:24).

Most of us will do whatever we can to meet the standards and criteria of success that others expect. We will use all of our effort to avoid the fears and insecurities which come from the feeling that we have failed and that we have been judged accordingly. When we enter into a relationship with Jesus, this self effort does not automatically leave us. It is 'the stuff' that the process of sanctification is focused on. It lives in the realm of our inner

WHEN WE RELY ON THIS SELF EFFORT AS CHRISTIANS THE BIBLE CALLS THIS 'WORKS OF THE FLESH'.

secret kingdom. When we rely on this self effort as Christians the Bible calls this *works of the flesh*. The ongoing pursuit of these *works of the flesh* result is a works based theology. That is, my effort will secure my righteousness, peace and God's favour.

Who will deliver me? was Paul's cry. It is our cry too. Paul's answer was that deliverance was through Jesus Christ. That is, what God does for people. Paul had to teach the Galatian church to hold to this place of deliverance. He found the Galatians reverting to self effort for their deliverance. That is, what they could do for God (Galatians 3:1-5).

When church leaders and congregations unwittingly follow the Galatian example they create behavioural standards that people respond to with on the basis of *should, have to, need to, expected to*. They believe that God's approval and man's approval will be secured by their effort. Again, Williams notes:

Evangelical churches preach a gospel of justification by faith, but often live a gospel of justification by works. As a result they are incredibly religious. They tell people that God loves them unconditionally, yet at the same time, pile conditions on them before including them in their fellowship... The hidden agenda is what people must do for God rather than what God wants to do for people. This blurring of unconditional and conditional love makes us crazy... By living out the gospel of justification by works the church merely apes our larger culture.[3]

In part, this situation is created because the church is focused on the narrower gospel of salvation rather than the broader gospel of the Kingdom of God. The gospel of salvation is often presented in terms of what I must do to be right with God more than what God can and will do in our lives when we place our faith and trust in Him. Justification is described as, 'just as if I had never sinned'. The emphasis of this description is on my sin and my behaviour. Equally problematic is the phrase, 'justification by faith'. Coined by Martin Luther it was used as a rally cry against the prevalent works based theology of the day. The phrase was underpinned by Romans 10:9-10:

...that if you confess with your mouth Jesus as Lord, and believe in your heart that God raised Him from the dead, you shall be saved; for with the heart man believes, resulting in righteousness, and with the mouth he confesses, resulting in salvation.

The danger in this phrase, 'justification by faith' is twofold: First, it narrows Paul's theology of justification onto our faith, at the exclusion or detriment of God's part in our regeneration (being born again). Second, it focusses on what we do to be born again, inadvertently creating an understanding that the Christian life is about what we do. We have our part to play but God's part is far bigger and more significant. Often, our experiences of salvation lead us to be more focused on what we did – repent and believe – rather than focus on what God has achieved through the Cross. One of the greatest consequences is that many Christians miss the radical nature of grace.[4]

Paul's theology of justification is about God's action in making people righteous, through pouring into their hearts love towards God (Romans 3:21-26) declaring:

But now apart from the Law the righteousness of God has been manifested, being witnessed by the Law and the Prophets, even the righteousness of God through faith in Jesus Christ for all those who believe; for there is no distinction; for all have sinned and fall short of the glory of God, being justified as a gift by His grace through the redemption which is in Christ Jesus; whom God displayed publicly as a propitiation in His blood through faith. This was to demonstrate His righteousness, because in the forbearance of God He passed over the sins previously committed; for the demonstration, I say, of His righteousness at the present time, that He might be just and the justifier of the one who has faith in Jesus.[4]

WHEN WE ARE RELEASED TO BE WHO GOD CREATED US TO BE, HIS LIFE IS RELEASED THOUGH US.

When we are released to be who God created us to be, His life is released through us. Then His Kingdom is both expressed and built in the communities in which we live.

Unfortunately our predisposition to performance and self effort keeps us from embracing the truth that our whole Christian life must be founded in the deep abiding knowledge of our total acceptance by God. When it comes to medical diagnosis of physical ailments we know that a superficial diagnosis can be fatal. If we think we have a skin infection when we really have a melanoma we can pay the ultimate price. The presence and power of self effort to remedy the fear and insecurities created by our response to a performance based life style is like cancer. Yet we can limp through this life with a low grade experience of the glorious gospel of Jesus Christ because we accept that, like everyone else, we have to protect ourselves in a hostile world. To continue the medical metaphor we are applying an ointment when God wants to perform surgery. Reliance on self effort has to be removed. It is carnal. It is destructive and it opposes the work of the Spirit. Yet it masquerades as acceptable because we see others being rewarded for 'their performance'.

Drawing from Proverbs 30: 21-22, Kris Vallotton characterises our position so well when he writes:

A pauper is born into insignificance. As he grows up he learns through life that he has no value and his opinions don't really matter. Therefore, when he becomes a king, he is important to the world around him but still he feels insignificant in the kingdom that lies within him.[5]

So, what is the pauper to do with what he has built on the inside when he wants to take his place in the world as one of the sons of God?

As I was explaining the theme of this book to someone in my congregation they responded, somewhat cheekily, by saying "So you are telling me that I no longer have to come to church, or pray, or to read my Bible?" I said, "That's right, you no longer have to, but... if you have really grasped how accepted you are by God and what He has done and wants to do for you then you will want to do those things".

If there are areas in our lives with God where our primary motivation is a feeling, sense or belief that we should, have to, need to, or are expected to do anything, then we are captive to a performance based culture in that area of our lives. In the next chapter I want to explore four things that may well help us to allow God to remove this cancer in our Christian life.

FOUR
THINGS
TO
CONSIDER

I myself do nothing. The Holy Spirit accomplishes all things through me.

WILLIAM BLAKE

Four Things to Consider

I came to faith in a blaze of God's glory. My conversion was radical, dynamic and powerful. Upon reflection I can now see that the strength of my personality, sharply trained mind and leadership gift presented me well. Before coming to faith I had been at university for five years. I graduated at the top of my year with a first class honours degree. While still not an academic, I had learned how to present my thoughts in a way that worked in the Department of Social Studies at Sydney University in the late seventies. I had developed strong analytical and critical skills that allowed me to debate the point to my advantage.

I believe that I was probably called by God around the age of eight but at the time had no idea that was the case. The gift of leadership had been with me through sport and then in youth groups. While in high school I was part of a small organising committee that pursued and broke the world record for marathon soccer playing twice, when I was 18 and 19. I was the leader of the student body in the Social Studies Department when at university.

After giving my life to Jesus I quickly, enthusiastically and passionately gave myself to the life of the congregation Phil Pringle was leading. I was asked to lead a small group after being a Christian for only six months. I attended the first year of the Bible college in Phil's church...and graduated in joint first place with my friend Mark Kelsey. I was making a difference in people's lives, adding value through my counselling skills and leadership gift. The church had entered into a stage of quick growth through 1982 – 1986. I was swept along with all God was doing.

By the time Lyn and I were back in Sydney after planting the church in Canberra we had been Christians for six years. We were now involved with Phil and others in not only building the local church but also in developing a fledgling movement of churches called Christian City

Church. These were exciting, exhilarating and fruitful days surrounded by young, vibrant and enthusiastic followers of Jesus. Together we were experiencing success and making a difference for the glory of God.

Looking back, I can see that I was honoured, encouraged and given incredible opportunity. I knew I was saved and justified but I hadn't had revelation of my adoption by God. I therefore responded to the extraordinary personal and corporate success of God's work at this time in a way that fed my performance orientation. Indicators and markers of success were upper most in my mind. I was being trapped and becoming a captive of comparison, numbers and an identity based on performance.

In Luke 4:18 Jesus says of Himself that He is anointed to proclaim release to the captives and to set the prisoners free. Kris Vallotton[1] makes a good distinction between prisoners and captives. Prisoners are people whom the judge has sent to prison. Captives are people who have been captured in a battle and held as prisoners of war. The spiritual equivalent is that a prisoner is someone who has sin and/or forgiveness issues in their life, and a captive is someone who has believed a lie.

My interest is in those who are captives to the performance base of our culture and how their response to this culture is expressed in their Christian lives. As already discussed, we respond to pressure to perform differently. We believe lies, take on hurts and receive wounds in the battles of life that, in turn, create fears and insecurities in us. There is no one solution for all. However, there are key areas to think and pray about that will position us with the Holy Spirit – our Counsellor – to find what He wants to do to set us free.

ACCEPTANCE AND PERFORMANCE

There are varying degrees, ways and places that we become captive to a performance based Christian life. It can be helpful to discover these by contrasting what a performance based mind-set is against an acceptance based mind-set.

Performance defines itself on the basis of what I do, how well I do it and what I gain from doing it. Acceptance defines itself on the basis of whose I am and who I am in Christ.

We live in a world that is obsessed with performance. Recently in Australia there was a television advertisement for a certain brand of whisky. A famous Australian cricketer was featured and he said of himself and the number of runs he scored: *numbers - they haunt me and define me.* This is true for students, teachers, sales people, church leaders, company executives, factory workers, in fact in just about any area of life.

In the performance mind-set, love, affirmation and inclusion are drawn out of effectiveness, that is, how well I am doing. In the acceptance mind-set, love, affirmation and inclusion are drawn out of significance, that is, what Jesus does for us.

> IN THE PERFORMANCE MIND-SET, LOVE, AFFIRMATION AND INCLUSION ARE DRAWN OUT OF EFFECTIVENESS, THAT IS, HOW WELL I AM DOING..

The values of this world would tie a person's acceptance to their performance. Sporting heroes, entertainment celebrities, political and business leaders find acceptance when they perform, and obscurity when they do not. The Kingdom of God keeps acceptance and performance separate. The Bible says, while I was a sinner – that is, ineffective in loving God – Christ died for me. Jesus thought I was significant enough to die for and He fully accepted me. Unfortunately, I observe evidence in church life and culture which, like the kingdoms of this world, tie a person's acceptance to their performance. Maybe a little unconsciously or unwittingly; certainly with no malice intended. However, the modelling is powerful and for those who are yet to be set free from the fear and insecurity associated with performance it becomes a powerful, seducing trap. The internal conflicts for the believer, and particularly leaders, are strong, confusing and powerful. Internally a conflict can exist between the importance of God and His place in our lives and a desire for more, bigger, better and breakthrough to meet the unquenchable thirst for significance. Pick me. Notice me. Listen to me. Spend time with me. Include me.

Performance, as it tries to avoid failure, is fuelled by fear anxiety, insecurity and worry. Acceptance as it embraces love, is fuelled by an authentic gospel that focusses our whole dependence on what God wants to do for us. Graham Cooke[2] writes:

Issues where we feel inadequate or insecure test us in our ability to depend on God. In those situations we usually fall into the trap of trying to prove ourselves, becoming locked in performance Christianity. And yet the Holy Spirit, in those moments, is trying to establish our dependence on God. Our test is to learn how to translate our insecurity into vulnerability towards God.

So, it can be said performance is concerned with:

a. **Having to deliver** characterized by: what do I have to do, helping God, judging others and defending self.

b. **Competition** characterised by: comparison with others, avoiding failure at another's expense, and personal best never being good enough.

c. **Striving** characterised by: things never being good enough, being driven, panic attacks and believing that the answers we seek and the mysteries we encounter are hidden from us and always just out of reach.

d. **An achieved** theology characterised by: ideas of God rewarding and punishing, being favoured and blessed on the basis of earning it, and wrestling with shame and guilt because failure is my responsibility and I need to do something about it.

Acceptance, however, is concerned with:

a. **God is love** characterised by: revelation knowledge of His goodness, mercy, grace, kindness, compassion and patience.

b. **Being adopted** characterised by: what we see and hear of God as our father.

c. **Our inheritance** characterised by: freedom, prosperity, supernatural power for salvation, healing and deliverance, sanctification and faith, hope and love.

d. **Rest** characterised by: His peace, His purposes and believing that the answers we seek and mysteries we encounter are hidden for us so that we can learn more about God and His ways.

e. **A received theology** characterised by: the pursuit of who He is, who we are in Him and our response to what He has done and is doing.

A most powerful illustration of these thoughts revolves around who is driving the motor bike and who is in the side car. A received theology places Jesus on the motor bike and us in the side car. An achieved theology wants to share the two positions depending on what level of fear and insecurity is being experienced.

Performance looks for resolution, growth and transformation through self-effort in a flesh led response. Acceptance looks for resolution, growth and transformation through abiding in the Word and beholding the glory of God – a spirit led response.

Faith is the product of surrender, not striving. Faith comes when we honour what God is doing and join ourselves to that, not trying to make things happen or carrying responsibility not given to us by God. Faith is found in peace and rest, not struggle.

Self-effort will result in striving and struggling. It includes trying to manage people's responses to us and proving that what we believe is right. It is concerned with protecting self and may be motivated

FAITH IS THE PRODUCT OF SURRENDER NOT STRIVING.

by the fear of man. The fear of man is part of a religious mind-set and leads us to eat at the table of public opinion instead of the table of obedience. It often is underpinned by unbelief, scepticism and cynicism.

The Christian life is not about self-effort. It is learning to abide (John 15:5) and behold (2 Corinthians 3:18), knowing that our minds need to be renewed (Romans 12:2) and our lives transformed for kingdom living. Jesus wants to teach us how to remain (abide) in the things God has done for us and to reflect on (behold) who God has been for us. On the other hand our spiritual enemies are trying to get us to rely on our self-effort (James 1:23–25).

These ideas are cogently illustrated in David's encounter with Goliath (1 Samuel 17). Goliath, like the devil's tactics against us, accused David through disdain, curses and presenting an image of what defeat would look like. "Who do you think you are?" "You don't have what it takes."

David's response was to say, "Hey, it's not about me, it's about God, His power and the fact that I am His servant."

David chose a reality based on who God was and who he was in God. He reflected on (beheld) the lion and bear encounters and chose to remain (abide) in the truth of those encounters. He did not allow Goliath's taunts to enter his heart. Another way of saying this is that he went to where God was for him. That is, within his inner secret kingdom where his knowledge of God was totally real to him. He refused to go to places where God was not. Those places of doubt, unbelief, anxiety, fear and insecurity brought about by the circumstances.

The internal stances we take are more important than our circumstances in determining the outcomes of life. The journey of life can be a voyage of mercy. While we are positioned in Christ and have everything pertaining to life and death, our experience is one of attaining all that this position offers. The Promised Land was given little by little. We develop and grow by increasing our weight-bearing capacity; by building our inner secret kingdom into the ways of God. We need to bear up under character and purity building experiences so that we can step into greater risk-taking opportunities and move in great power. God's position is that according to our weight-bearing capacity He will reveal more and more to us. The pace is greatly influenced by our willingness to obey without analysis or dissection.

David's internal stance was strengthened and continually transformed by *abiding* and *beholding*. He had three main stances in the midst of the circumstances of Goliath's bullying that came from his abiding and beholding.

The first stance was: 'In the name of the Lord'. Romans 5:10–11 declares that we are reconciled to God. This means that we have become friends after an estrangement. We are totally compatible with God. As my good friend Graeme Cooke declares3, God is no longer interested in what is wrong, but in what is missing. Because we are reconciled we have authority in life and will be saved through life's circumstances, both because of what Jesus has done for us, and because of who we are in Christ. So we can also declare with assurance that life will change because of the name of the Lord as we reflect on and remain in the truth of our reconciliation.

The second stance David took was 'The Lord will deliver'. Romans 8:14-17 declares that we can call God our 'Daddy'[4]. There comes a point where we exchange the faith of a servant for the faith of a son. (I will address this in more detail in the next chapter). We have sonship not by struggling legalistically up the rungs of a ladder but because the Holy Spirit has come down the ladder and lifted us up into

> **THERE COMES A POINT WHERE WE EXCHANGE THE FAITH OF A SERVANT FOR THE FAITH OF A SON.**

the unending flow of love in the Godhead. It is Jesus who has opened the way by which slaves become sons. Paul also says that it is the Holy Spirit who applies the benefit of the finished work of Christ to our lives. So, we can confidently say the Lord will deliver us as we reflect on and remain in the truth of our adoption.

The third stance David took was that 'The battle is the Lord's'. Romans 8:31-39 powerfully presents this truth in the context of who God is for us. Knowledge of who God is for us is not to be determined by our circumstances. Regardless of what we are experiencing at any moment in time we are the beloved (be-loved) of God (Romans 1:7, Philippians 2:12). God wants to give to us. It is what He wants to do for us, much more than what we can do for Him. However, when circumstances and relationships scream at us that we are failing, hopeless, no good, not good enough, inadequate or haven't done enough we can easily return to a performance based mentality and look to our own self-effort for the resolution. Being loved by God needs to be at the very core of our existence. Our acceptance by the Father is foundational to our Christian life. Our sense of acceptance needs to be sustained otherwise we will go back to striving to earn God's acceptance through our achievements. So we can be certain the Lord is fighting for us, with us, as we reflect on and remain in the truth of being accepted and loved.

A full experience of Christian living is based on what God does. Our experience of growing up in a performance oriented culture may result in the belief and values that much of life is about what I do. David did something: he fought and defeated Goliath. His internal stance, in his inner secret kingdom, was on God's ability and nature, not on his own ability and effort. David had won the internal battle and exchanged the belief that self-effort is primary, with the truth that God is primary.

When a performance based mentality is not clothed in the deep reality of God's acceptance the resulting self-effort creates nothing but pride or despair. It measures adequacy of gifts and skill which is self-absorbed and self-centred. Reliance on performance is a dead end street as it rarely opens up the door of creativity. It deadens our interaction with the core of our soul and its spirituality. It narrows life to measuring value and worth with numbers. Friendship is rarely its prize. Criticism and judgment readily become its bedfellows. As a result its creations are cynicism, scepticism, fear and doubt. It seeks to live on the shallowness of results, while stifling love because of its inherent need to avoid fear and insecurity.

Performance focusses on successfully achieving standards. The motivations for performance are varied but our response to the inevitable failures is what affects the way we live. What message does failure bring to a person's sense of value, worth, dignity and being loved and accepted? How does the individual compensate emotionally and mentally for times when the messages are negative? To handle the negative messages, what coping mechanisms are being put in place and what foundations are they being built on? Where does the work of demonic forces in accusation, fear, anxiety, shame and guilt play its part in forming these foundations? How do these foundations then resist the development of faith, hope and love in a person's inner secret kingdom? How easily do we accept the truths of the Christian life intellectually through information and inspiration, and neglect the real spiritual work of allowing the Word of God, with the Holy Spirit, to birth truth deep in our souls?

The rich freedom of the Christian life, associated with a transformed mind, through abiding and beholding, and the experiences of the supernatural await the pursuit of hungry hearts. We can no longer allow the whispers of truth that reach our inner secret kingdom to be lost in the shadows of our dominant thoughts generated by the poverty of our life experiences.

As I conclude this section take time to consider those areas where you may be influenced by a performance based mind-set. Continue your voyage of mercy by asking the Holy Spirit how He wants to help you unravel its influence in the way you live life. What truth does He want to reveal to you so that you can walk in freedom? Take time to reflect on these things over the coming days and weeks and remain in this truth. Then be prepared for circumstances to present themselves so that you can take your new stance. Have confidence in a good God who wants to do good things for everyone.

GOD'S ROLE

Many of us are under a spell as we try to perfect by performance what we have received by the Spirit (Galatians 3:1-5). We listen to the word of God through our performance based mind-set without even knowing it.

Mark 9:2-7 recounts the transfiguration of Jesus. Moses was representing the law. Elijah was representing the prophets. Yet, God said 'listen to Jesus'. As New Testament believers we are not to listen to 'the spirit of the law' that promotes works and sacrifice to gain right standing with God. Nor are we to listen to 'the spirit of the prophets' that emphasises judgment and correction. Rather we are to listen to Jesus who promotes what God does for us with love, acceptance, grace and mercy.

Many of God's people see themselves as sinners more than saints. In Ephesians 1:1 Paul writes to saints and not sinners. The problem with seeing ourselves as sinners is that we listen to the implication that we are prone to do wrong. The truth is that our new nature in Christ is righteousness and therefore we are saints (Romans 6:11, 8:1-2) whether we acknowledge it or not. This is important because if we see ourselves as sinners, we will struggle to obtain through performance, what we have already received through our salvation. When we listen to the spirit of the law and/or prophets we reinforce the notion of being a sinner and the need for performance.

In reality our sinful past no longer exists. Sin's power to destroy us is itself destroyed by the superior reality of forgiveness. Bill Johnson[5], writing about himself observes:

I struggled for so many years with this truth. Shame and discouragement were close friends of mine. I would counter such feelings with more prayer, study, and reading about the lives of great men and women of God from the past. Yet, my problem wasn't solved, even though I was doing what most would counsel me to do... My shame was over my humanity and my discouragement was over who I wasn't. At some point I actually had to believe that what King Jesus did was enough. It sounds so simple now. My shame quietly

SIN'S POWER TO DESTROY US IS ITSELF DESTROYED BY THE SUPERIOR REALITY OF FORGIVENESS.

denied His atoning work. My discouragement dishonoured the sufficiency of the King's promises.

To break a performance based mind-set we need to listen to the following truths:

a. God does not ask us to do anything He is not prepared to do Himself; *and,*

b. Everything He asks us to do He originates in us

For example, Mark 12:28-31 sets out the two great commandments that are both based in love: loving God and loving others. However, 1 John 4:19 declares *We love, because He first loved us.* That is, we have a capacity to love that comes from God himself. When we come to love God and others we simply need to access the love we know God has for us. When this happens, we can adequately love God and others. We struggle in the expression of love when we either choose to go to places of rejection and self-defence, or, when we try to love in our own strength. This well eventually runs dry.

We grow in our capacity to love God and others in two ways. First, as we remain in, and reflect on, the love we know God has for us, it grows and expands. Second, we need to increase our capacity to receive God's love. We are loved fully by a God who describes Himself the following way:

The Lord, the Lord God compassionate and gracious, slow to anger, and abounding in lovingkindness and truth; who keeps lovingkindness for thousands, who forgives iniquity, transgression and sin... (Exodus 34:6-7).

Yet our capacity to receive God's love is hindered by many things. Having a low opinion of ourselves (when you don't agree with God's view of you it is not helpful to the Holy Spirit), or seeing ourselves as a failure. God does not change the way He feels about us when we fail. We are also hindered by measuring the value of our life on the basis of performance rather than His acceptance of us through Jesus. We tend not to see God the way He is, as much as we see Him the way we are. For example, when we are performance oriented we see God as a judge who according to some behavioural standard assesses us as wrong, bad and unworthy. Paradoxically we often treat others this way because we are *being like God*. However, if we are acceptance oriented we see God as merciful and wanting to help us with what's missing. The more we see God the way He really is, the more we become like Him (1 John 3:2). The only evidence that we share God's DNA is how we love God and others.

If our capacity to receive God's love is at ten percent, then from God's point of view we are missing out by 90 percent. He does not want us to operate at a minimum. He is not a God of measure. He is a God of fullness. Therefore, He is relentless in helping us to increase our capacity by discovering who we are in Christ and what we have received as our inheritance. How does this occur?

...IF WE ARE ACCEPTANCE ORIENTED WE SEE GOD AS MERCIFUL WHO WANTS TO HELP US WITH WHAT'S MISSING.

We were once slaves of sin but now we are slaves of righteousness. Our thought life must support that reality. When we agree with the devil we empower him. When we empower him, he devours. On the other hand, agreeing with God empowers us. This involves repentance which ultimately means to change the way we think. We need repentance that affects our thought life (Romans 12:2) and redirects our heart towards a God who forgives. We begin to agree with God. This is how we cooperate with the Lord to increase our capacity to receive and live in His love.

So, when we are called to regard one another as more important than ourselves (Philippians 2:3), we can do this because the Lord was prepared to do it first (Philippians 2:5-8). Loving others is not a question of self-effort it is recognising that the Lord never asks us to do anything He is not prepared to do Himself. As we live from an acceptance mind-set we realise that all we need is found in Him and what He has done or us. No longer is life about what we do but how we live in what He has done and is now doing for us.

> **NO LONGER IS LIFE ABOUT WHAT WE DO BUT HOW WE LIVE IN WHAT HE HAS DONE AND IS NOW DOING FOR US.**

FORMED FOR KINGDOM WORKS

When we cannot break from natural things to give birth to spiritual things, it results in us giving birth to lame things[6]. This is a very powerful statement and principle in the Kingdom of God. In this context it has two applications.

Firstly if we can't break from natural mind-sets those mind-sets will determine our identity and our future. My personal voyage of mercy resulted in the realisation that my performance based mind-set with its associated fears and insecurities meant that I was susceptible to being led by my soul – a natural thing. My performance was creating my identity and I was relying on these two to bring me acceptance.

The essential elements and order of a person's salvation experience are calling, conviction, regeneration (being born again), justification and adoption. I have found that many Christians, including myself, neglect the element of adoption where we enter into the confident assurance that God is our Father and we are His children. (This is described more fully in the following chapter.) However, when we neglect pursuing the revelation of adoption we pay a great price. We carry inside our secret inner kingdom the tendency to revert to being slaves of a performance orientation and its associated fear.

Our spiritual enemies tempt us to believe that the Christian life is about what we do. In Exodus 3:11 Moses asks *"Who am I that I should go to Pharaoh, and that I should bring the children of Israel out of Egypt?"* This question focusses on himself, his qualities, his attributes, his activity. God appears to ignore Moses' question when He answers in Exodus 3:12, *"Certainly I will be with you."* God answers Moses' question of "Who am I?" with "You are the man God goes with." In other words, "Moses, it is not about you, it is about me. Your identity is in the fact that you are mine. That is, fully accepted and adopted by Me."

The devil attacked God's identity in Genesis 3. He attacked Jesus' identity in Luke 4. We can be sure he will attack our identity, and our greatest point of weakness is primarily in the area of performance. Without the revelation of adoption as sons we are vulnerable to being bewitched (Galatians 3:1-4). Paul powerfully writes in 2 Corinthians 1:8-9, *For we do not want you to be unaware, brethren, of our affliction which came to us in Asia, that we were burdened excessively, beyond our strength, so that we despaired even of life; indeed we had the sentence of death within ourselves SO THAT WE WOULD NOT TRUST IN OURSELVES, but in the God who raises the dead.* (Capitals are my emphasis)

Paul is as clear as he can be that under no circumstances would the Lord allow them to believe that it was up to them, their effort, their gifts, their anything. In fact the Lord was prepared to allow them to face deep inner turmoil, burdened excessively, beyond our strength, so that we despaired even of life... in order that they hold onto the truths of their adoption and resulting identity. It is a big deal to the Lord for those who are going to be used in power to know where the source of the power comes from.

In contrast to our natural mind-sets and personal performance forming our identity, we need our identity to be based on revelation and knowledge of our acceptance in God. It is out of this identity, founded on God's acceptance, we bear fruit and perform. This is a spirit-led position.

Romans 8:14 declares: *For all who are being led by the Spirit of God, these are the sons of God.*

In summary,

Performance → Identity → Acceptance (being soul led)
Acceptance → Identity → Performance (being spirit led)

If we can't break from natural things (being led by the soul) to give birth to spiritual things (being led by the Spirit) then we give birth to lame things – a Christian life that is not experiencing all the freedom and inheritance Jesus won for us. To live in all that Jesus has for us we must be prepared to have the parts of us, and places in us, that are performance oriented to be removed through revelation of our acceptance and adoption. Like Moses we need to transition from the Christian life being about what we do, to what God does through us.

The second application of this principle is in relation to what we give birth to in the area of Kingdom work. The only way to consistently carry out works is to view reality from God's perspective[7]. Kingdom works result in fruit that brings glory to God (John 5:1-11). We need to live from acceptance so that we bear fruit (perform) and glorify God.

The topic of Kingdom works is very large. For the purposes of this discussion I will somewhat simplistically say that they include representing (or re-presenting) Jesus (2 Corinthians 5:20), living in His character and power (1 John 2:6) and, doing greater works than Jesus (John 14:12). These are possible because Jesus taught us to pray Your Kingdom come, Your will be done, on earth as it is in heaven (Matthew 9:10-10).

To do these works consistently we need to view reality from God's perspective. To view reality from God's perspective we need to learn to live from His world, the invisible world, toward the visible world, what we see in our circumstances and relationships. The renewed mind reflects the reality of another world. A world from God's perspective. Romans 8:6 says, *For the mind-set on the flesh is death, but the mind-set on the spirit is life and peace.*

THE RENEWED MIND REFLECTS THE REALITY OF ANOTHER WORLD.

This is one of the reasons Paul prays as he does: *I pray that the eyes of your heart will be enlightened, so that you will know what is the hope of His calling, which are the riches of the glory of His inheritance in the saints and what is the surpassing greatness of His power to us who believe.* (Ephesians 1:18-19)

Paul recognises the absolute necessity and priority of our having a right view of our adoption the *hope of His calling*, our impact on the world *the riches of the glory of His inheritance in the saints*, who God is and what He, not us, is capable of *surpassing greatness of His power towards us who believe*. The reality we live in determines the life we will lead.

Jesus' primary means of bringing His Kingdom to earth was proclamation and demonstration; the message then the ministry. The two disciples on the road to Emmaus declared Jesus was *powerful in word and deed* (Luke 24:19). The apostles continued this pattern of words and works. Peter in Acts 2 and 3, Phillip in Acts 8:5-3 and Paul in Romans 15:18 and 1 Corinthians 2:1-5 demonstrate this. All these kingdom works and assignments were accomplished by men who believed it was not what we can do for God but what God can do through us.

When we can't break from seeing reality through the limitations of our effort, experience and rational thinking, to give birth to demonstrations of power, signs and wonders, we give birth to a Christian life that is mediocre in comparison to what is promised in the New Testament. For me I have arrived at a time in my life when I will tell people how great the gospel is *and* demonstrate it through experience. *Taste and see that the Lord is good* (Psalm 34:8).

THE ROLE OF THE HOLY SPIRIT

Many Christians have the creed: "I believe in God the Father, I believe that Jesus is the Son of God, but I wonder about the Holy Spirit." Yet, Jesus said it was good that He went to the Father so that the Holy Spirit would come (John 16:7). It is not my intention to give a full and comprehensive theology of the Holy Spirit. However, it is vital that comment is made on the Holy Spirit's role in the voyage of mercy when it comes to performance and acceptance.

The Holy Spirit was sent to reveal what is beyond our comprehension (1 Corinthians 2:9-10). If we focus on the natural realm, that is, our work, our effort, our responsibility, or what others think it is like we are on the AM band of the radio. If we focus on the realm of

THE HOLY SPIRIT WAS SENT TO REVEAL WHAT IS BEYOND OUR COMPREHENSION

the spirit, that is, the ways of God, what He is saying, His view of us and reality, then we are on the FM band of the radio. When we are on the AM band we cannot receive the FM band. For example, the Holy Spirit gives wisdom and revelation, not strategy as we know it. He is concerned with working with us and not us working for Him based on our commitment to be responsible. If we live on the AM band (at a soul level) we forfeit the benefits from being on the FM band (the Spirit's level). 1 Corinthians 3:21-23 illustrates this by declaring that what we have is not on the basis of which leader we follow but because we belong to Jesus.

The Holy Spirit is the source of revelation. Revelation removes a veil so we can see what is already there. It does not create knowledge. The Holy Spirit will stir our affection for unseen things as it is His role to disclose what we need. Our assignments from heaven are so big that we need access to His knowledge. Deuteronomy 29:29 says

"The secret things belong to the Lord our God, but the things revealed belong to us AND TO OUR SONS FOREVER..." (Capitals my empahasis)

Therefore, what Enoch, David, and all the legends of the Bible and church history knew, is still available. Much has been lost because it wasn't handed on but it is still waiting to be found. We just need to ask the Holy

Spirit and He will equip and empower us for the things He is inviting us to do with Him (Matthew 7:11, 1 John 3:21-22, John 14:13-14).

The reception of information from the Holy Spirit is interesting. For people serving God from a performance based mind-set, information is seen as being useful to help performance and enhance achievements. For those who see themselves more as friends of God, living in His acceptance, they are receiving secrets that have a time and place to be talked about. The receipt of revelation increases the responsibility of the one to whom it is given. This is why Jesus taught in parables. A person's hunger, thirst and desperation will unlock mysteries – things God has hidden for us, not from us. God does not bring revelation prematurely as He will hold us accountable for the way we respond to these revelations[8]. Every mystery is an invitation to an encounter with God. Every revelation is attended to with an experience of God. Our delight is to be in His presence not in the outcomes of His presence.

OUR DELIGHT IS TO BE IN HIS PRESENCE NOT IN THE OUTCOMES OF HIS PRESENCE.

The Holy Spirit looks for intimacy in the context of a fresh vibrant relationship. Faith comes by hearing (Romans 10:17) more than it does from having heard. Isaac is very pleased about this truth. Abraham heard that he was to sacrifice Isaac. However, the Lord had more to say to Abraham about this matter. The fresh instruction from God was to sacrifice the lamb caught in the thicket instead of Isaac. In this instance, faith came from hearing and what was previously heard was no longer relevant. Those of God's people who are performance orientated can live from what was heard in the last crisis and not from an intimate daily relationship with the Lord.

OUR
VIEW OF
GOD

Whatever God's dreams about man may be,
it seems certain it cannot come true unless man cooperates.

STELLA TERRILL MANN

Leadership is both a skill and an art. It is something you can be born with and it definitely needs to be developed. Development invariably occurs on the job and requires self awareness, reflection and a desire to change.

Leadership is expressed under the scrutiny and gaze of others. Leaders make mistakes, and those following are left with choices about how to respond when this happens. Leaders who have strongly identified with the performance base of our culture can find it a challenge to embrace mistakes as an opportunity to grow and learn.

Until 1996 there had been enough 'success' around my life to balance the negative impact of my mistakes. During 1996-97 my world came crashing in around me. During this time thirty percent of the congregation I was leading left, and thirty percent of my staff resigned for unrelated reasons. In certain quarters there was much criticism of me, both personally and of the way I was leading the church. I felt deeply betrayed. I wanted to resign and retreat to lick my wounds in isolation. I lost my confidence as a leader. I was no longer leading through vision.

I experienced a great sense of failure, despair and anger during this time. My leadership was focused on trying to preserve what was left and defending myself in the face of hostile criticism from those leaving. I felt rejected by men and somewhat abandoned by God. I questioned my performance and found very few places of affirmation.

IT WAS DURING THESE TWO YEARS THAT I RETREATED INTO LIVING MY LIFE THROUGH SELF EFFORT.

It was during these two years that I retreated into living my life through self effort. In the absence of knowing by revelation that God loved and accepted me I used the strength of my giftedness and temperament to stay sane, and in control. While my mind reasoned that, 'God works all things together for good', my emotional response was to do as much as I could to help Him. Consequently, I led the church by exercising my leadership gift and the development of programmes, trusting these would bring stability and growth. I continued to pursue spiritual disciplines of prayer, Bible reading, fasting and meditation. Yet, with hindsight, the purpose was to perform in a way I thought would please God and therefore bless what I was doing.

For me now, the simplicity of the truth of God's acceptance is blindingly obvious. However, as the next chapter will patently describe, it has not always been like this for me. The deconstruction of the performance lie was not pleasant to say the least. My response to my failures, perceived and real, created and developed a range of fears and insecurities that impacted the way I lived my Christian life.

DECEPTION ONLY BECOMES APPARENT WHEN THE LIGHT OF TRUTH IS ALLOWED TO PENETRATE IT.

When a lie is deconstructed, the truth seems so simple. More significantly, a truth believed purely on an intellectual level appears simple and obvious. It is only when this truth is tested through the realities of living, and found wanting in its application when lies are exposed, that it no longer seems simple. Deception only becomes apparent when the light of truth is allowed to penetrate it. Living in denial can be a beautiful thing!

A primary reason why Christians remain caught, to one degree or another, in a performance based mind-set is that the truth of who God really is, is resisted. Layers of lies and deception about how good God is have been formed in our subconscious and conscious minds. We are convinced these ideas represent the truth because when we are placed under pressure and challenged by circumstances or mystery, we capitulate and return to our underlying doubts and lies. Scepticism and cynicism are demanding enemies of truth while naivety results in the lazy and reluctant pursuit of deep abiding truth.

The deconstruction process began for me as I studied one of Jesus' parables, a Gospel story and Mark Stibbe's book *From Orphans to Heirs*[1]. I had accepted in my head the truths contained in the parable, the story and the book. Following inspirational preaching and writing of others, I had thought these truths had become ingrained in me. However, who we are when we are under pressure is who we really are. When under pressure, an honest personal examination of my behaviour and thought life revealed I was still seeing God as I was, not who He was (1 John 3:2). My lies and doubts about who God really was only became apparent as I allowed the light of truth to come in. My deeply held views of God only changed as I chose to let Him be who He said He would be in the most painful and challenging of circumstances and mystery. God leads us to revelation, and to assignments that are so grand that at first there is a fight to receive them and appropriate them.

I have found that the primary purpose of revelation and truth is an encounter with God, not knowledge, although this is an outcome. Let me illustrate this with a discussion on baptism. Baptism is symbolic of no longer living for ourselves but God. There are two different types of baptism in the Old Testament represented by the Red Sea and the Jordan River. A Red Sea baptism is characterised by an enemy chasing, circumstances creating no way out and entering the experience out of necessity, not willingly. At the time of this baptism the Israelites carried with them Egyptian riches, were strongly influenced by a foreign philosophy and only had a historical knowledge of God. The Jordan River baptism is characterised by preparing to chase the enemy, discerning the Lord's leading and demonstrating how to die to self and willingly entering the experience. At the time of this baptism, the Israelites had the Ark of the Covenant, a Priesthood and faith in a supernatural God.

WHENEVER RISK IS INVOLVED, STRONGHOLDS WILL BE EXPOSED.

In wanting to deconstruct the lie of performance, I was pursuing a Jordan River baptism, knowing this would expose strongholds in my thinking that needed to be transformed. Whenever risk is involved, strongholds will be exposed. Yet, as at the Jordan, I knew I needed answers that were beyond my human capacity. I required an encounter with God that genuinely shifted my Egyptian treasure of performance to carrying the undeniable truth and reality of God's acceptance of me. I was prepared to do whatever was necessary before seeing any change. I was willingly choosing to die to how I managed my fear and insecurity and how I was masking my incapability.

A PARABLE

We know Luke 15:11-32 as the parable of the prodigal son. However, more recent commentary is casting a new perspective on these Scriptures. The truth is that the subject of the story is the father, 'a certain man', not the prodigal son.

Verse 11 introduces the father. Verses 12 to 19 speak of the younger son's rebellion against the father. Verses 20 to 24 speak of the father's compassion. Verses 25 to 30 speak of the older son's anger toward the father. Verses 31 and 32 speak again of the father.

Interestingly, both sons had a wrong view of their father. Both sons ended up being slaves; the younger to sin and the older to the law. Yet only the younger son found his freedom. Let's look at the older son as an example of what it is to be performance orientated and how this impacts his view of the father.

The older son was a slave to law. His language gives away the condition of his heart. In verse 29 he cries *"all these years I've been slaving for you."* He sees his father as a task master. He is living not as a much loved son, but as a slave to perceived expectation. He goes on to say in verse 29, *"I have never disobeyed a command"*. He sees his father as a law giver – someone who is distant and to be feared. He is not living in a father/son relationship; he is living in a master/servant relationship. He goes on to declare, *"you never gave me a goat"*. You don't accept me as you do my brother. I've earned my acceptance but you have not given me any reward. The older son reveals his insecurity and is not even aware he is doing so. In verse 30, he reveals the depth of his heart's attitude by intimating that his father's favour should be earned not given on the basis of repentance. He declares "Performance, Dad, is the key to celebration, not your goodness."

I can't find words to describe how distressing it was to see myself in the older son. I was struck by the realisation that I want mercy when I do wrong but I would readily judge others when they were wrong. It is one thing to receive mercy – it is another to be able to give it. I believed the breaking of behavioural standards was to be judged. My childhood religion was based on this, and I treated myself and others, in my inner secret kingdom, this way. My love for others would be governed by their behaviour, and character performance, therefore I assumed this was who God was. Often instead of being conformed to the image of God we conform God to our image. However, God's love for us is governed by who He is, not who we are (Colossians 3:12-14). Because we tend to see God as we are, not as He is, deep inside I

...GOD'S LOVE FOR US IS GOVERNED BY WHO HE IS, NOT WHO WE ARE.

did not expect to receive mercy from God. Rather I was trying to avoid His judgment, and my own, through increased effort, responsibility and spiritual discipline.

Matthew 6:22-23 says: *The lamp of the body is the eye; if therefore your eye is clear, your whole body will be full of light. But if your eye is bad, your whole body will be full of darkness. If therefore the light that is in you is darkness, how great is the darkness!*

When you believe a lie is the truth then the darkness only increases. For example, I believed that God was judgmental. This is a lie because *mercy triumphs over judgment* (James 2:13). However, I believed the lie was the truth resulting in the increase of darkness through self effort and being bewitched (Galatians 3:1). When the basis of our evaluation is inaccurate or biased, but is assumed to be accurate, then every decision we make takes us further away from our goal. Trusting an error prone compass results in wrong conclusions but we believe they are right. We get further off track, but no matter how much effort we put in, things don't improve because the problem is in the compass not our effort.

There are places in our inner secret kingdom that are closer to darkness than they are to light. We can be Bible believing, faith filled, Spirit led people in some areas yet only one step away from darkness in other areas. For example, when we focus on what God hasn't done, we at best try to help Him through self effort or at worst become bitter and resentful towards Him. We legitimize our unbelief when we focus on what God hasn't done. The story of the pool of Bethesda (John 5:2) records what Jesus did, not all the things he didn't do or could have done. We need to focus our attention on what God is doing and move with Him. This attitude positions us for the next thing

RELIGION IS OBSESSED WITH WHAT IS WRONG. RELATIONSHIP IS ABSORBED WITH DISCOVERING WHAT IS MISSING.

God wants to do. Religion is obsessed with what is wrong. Relationship is absorbed with discovering what is missing (Proverbs 25:2).

The true nature of the father, and of God the Father, is revealed in this parable. Verse 20 shows the father to be patient, compassionate and demonstrative. Patient, because after being rejected he keeps a faithful vigil at the village gates (2 Peter 3:9). Compassionate, because his heart does not burn with indignation (Isaiah 30:15-18). Demonstrative, because He cannot help showing his feelings, showering affection on his son and treasuring intimacy (Ephesians 1:8; 1 John 3:1). It was this father who said to the eldest son – *"my child, you have always been with me, and all that is mine is yours."*

As I identified with the elder son, I listened to what the Father said to him. *"My child"*, words pregnant with position and possibilities, settling questions of inheritance and purpose. Words drawing me to intimacy and influencing my knowledge of acceptance. Words dispelling the position of a slave and expectation of a distant fearful God. Words that called me to understand what it was to be adopted.

"You have always been with me", compounding mystery and calling out to childhood memories of wanting to serve God. These words pointed

to the possibilities of the unimaginable and the need to embrace the lengths that God went to, for my affection to be centred on Him.

"All that is mine is yours", exploded into my awareness the possibilities of a life that makes a difference. These words re-ignited the fires of my previous supernatural experiences, allowing me to rediscover with the knowledge that we have been assigned to the realms of impossibility. Everything God has asked us to do and be is impossible. Heal the sick, raise the dead, cleanse lepers, and save the lost. Our assignment is to confront infirmities, afflictions and torments that face mankind. God wants us to enjoy His unlimited life and declares that nothing will be impossible for those who believe (Matthew 17:20). When we either assign the purposes of God to the past (that is the ascension gift ministries died with the apostles) or to the future (that is they are either for the millennium or heaven) we abdicate our responsibility to be the people God called us to be.

In the story of feeding the five thousand (Mark 6: 34-44), the disciples were reluctant to co-operate with Jesus to see a miracle. Jesus invited them to find an answer with Him but they were avoiding taking responsibility. They began by procrastinating (verse 35), leaving it till late in the day to raise the matter. They then tried to pass the buck (verse 36) by wanting the people to solve the problem themselves. Finally, they became anxious about how much it would cost to solve the problem because they were looking at the problem. Yet they didn't ask Jesus – the one who turned water into wine – for His solution; a solution of abundance that represented promised land living not wilderness living.

Ministry should not be reduced to gifts that comfort and lead. New Testament ministry is trusting the God who invades the impossible with the supernatural. That is why we must believe that we have a Father who acts on His statement that "All that is mine is yours"(Matthew 28:18-20; Ephesians 11:20-23; Colossians 2: 9-10). We can step into who God says we are and we will demonstrate who God really is.

A STORY

Fear and insecurity, no matter how they are established and developed in

FEAR AND INSECURITY...LEAD US TO MANAGE LIFE FROM OUR OWN RESOURCES.

us, lead us to manage life from our own resources. We rely on our will power, our emotional power and our mental power to deal with the lies, wounds and hurts of life. Performance based fear and insecurity build an inner secret kingdom that focusses on what I have, what I do and what others think of me. We believe we really need to earn what we get. Our emotional framework looks to earn the love we seek. From these places feelings are generated that require having our needs met, sometimes in a very driven and aggressive manner. These feelings are not at rest in love and affection. In these places we only accept measured doses of unconditional love and affection. Paradoxically, we resist the fullness of unconditional love and its associated intimacy because it requires full surrender.

To follow Jesus completely assumes that we fully exchange managing life from our own resources, to managing life from God's resources. We are to live by the power that comes from God and not by our will power, emotional power and mental power. Before asking Jesus to forgive our sin and come into our life, our inner secret kingdom was doing natural things and thinking natural thoughts (James 1:23; 1 Corinthians 2:14). When we start to follow Jesus, we can now choose to go to those places that are spiritual, places where we think and act according to the ways of the Spirit (Ephesians 4:17-24). The mistake we make is believing we can make our natural man more spiritual through greater effort and discipline in prayer, reading the Word and fasting. This only leads us to religion. The truth is that our natural man can't think spiritual thoughts. We can't make our natural man spiritual.

When we are born again we receive everything God has for us. We are never going to be more spiritual than we are right now (Ephesians 1:3). We are to live from, and grow, and develop these places in our secret inner kingdom where we know God's love, what He has done for us and rely on what He wants to do for us. For example, we don't become more loving by what we do; we absorb and accept the truth of His love so that it flows out of us. In this way our secret inner kingdom is being renewed in God's love, empowering us to receive His love and give it away. Our natural places of thinking and doing are displaced by the spiritual as God is at work. Now loving others is not about our ability, but about our acceptance that we are deeply loved.

When we live from the natural parts of our inner secret kingdom we pray, seeking the power of God to deliver us from our circumstances. When we live from the spiritual places of our inner secret kingdom we pray, seeking the presence of God for fellowship with Him,

IT HAS NOTHING TO DO WITH WHAT WE DO OR DON'T HAVE. IT HAS EVERYTHING TO DO WITH HIS LOVE FOR US.

to be with Him through the circumstances and into the answers. This approach to our voyage of mercy assumes a desire for deeper intimacy. However, to be intimate is to be utterly dependent on His willingness to give Himself to us. That is, He is giving Himself to us not because we deserve it, have earned it or are weak and miserable. It has nothing to do with what we do or don't have. It has everything to do with His love for us.

God is motivated by intimacy (1 John 4:8). The Lord is more interested in relationship with us than He is focused on our works, activity and tasks (Matthew 22:36-40). Intimacy is to abandon ourselves to God, giving up control of what matters most to us and embracing Jesus and all He wants for us. To be intimate with God is to place our total confidence and trust in someone we can't control but who is good and kind. It is being in love with God not just the idea of God. It is like learning to float where we have to let go of the side of the boat. We have to stop standing on the bottom, stop trying to tread water, and stop lifting up our head to see where we are going. The performance based mind-set in our inner secret kingdom cannot do this. You do not cast out the darkness. You turn the light on and light dispels the darkness. The performance mind-set has to be replaced with an acceptance based mind-set as illustrated in the story of Mary and Martha (Luke 10:28-42).

It is important to note that Martha was not corrected for service, rather the correction was because of distracted service. We are to do things for God (James 1:22-39) and bear fruit (John 15:1-11). Performance out of acceptance brings glory to God. However, when our performance becomes focused on what we are doing , having taken our eyes off Jesus, then it is distracted service.

For Martha, distracted service led firstly to worry (Luke 10:41). Worry is the fear of that which is important to us not happening. Worry takes us away from God because we are not trusting the one who said "cast all your cares upon me" (1 Peter 5:7) and "I will supply all your needs". (Philippians 4:19)

After worry, Martha becomes angry, *Don't you care that....* (Luke 10:40) She is now angry with the one person who cares for her more than anyone else. Then she commands the Lord to act, *"Then tell her to help me"* (Luke 10:40). We, like Martha, can try to use God to accomplish what we want. In the process we end up judging our brothers and sisters by our standards of service. Distracted service, if it is based on a performance oriented mind-set becomes service for ourselves, so that we will feel better trying to impress God and others.

Socially Mary was out of order. Traditionally, women were expected to prepare the meal and only men were in the room socialising, conversing and eating together. Everyone, including Mary and Jesus, knew she was not meant to be in the room. Being responsible has its place, but when it is task and performance focused and distracts us from intimacy with Jesus, it can be wrong. Jesus really only wants two things: intimacy and relationship. We were created for it (Genesis 2:15-25) and it is the centre piece of the two great commandments (Mark 12:28-31). Mary chose intimacy. It didn't just happen. Everything else in life will be taken away but being loved and giving love to the Lord will always remain. Mary's way of serving was accepted. It had two characteristics: sitting as close as she could, humbly at his feet; and listening with a hungry heart.

JESUS CAME NOT TO BE HOSTED BUT TO BE THE HOST.

Interestingly, on the day Jesus visited, there were two banquets. A banquet from Martha that Jesus did not order. And there was a banquet Jesus was serving that Mary participated in. Jesus came not to be hosted, but to be the host. It was not about what could be done for Him, but what He wanted to do for them. He came to be enjoyed, and to enjoy Him is to be His friend (John

15:12-14). We are to share His heart because the world is impacted by who we are, not by what we know. We are to learn how to let ourselves be deeply loved by God before we place too strong an emphasis on acquiring knowledge by doing things.

CELEBRATING OUR SPIRITUAL ADOPTION

I've recently watched very good friends adopt an Ethiopian child. As we walked the journey with them I realised that all children are adopted on the initiation and at the expense of the adoptive parents. It is not the child's achievements but parental grace that creates this new family and a loving relationship.

During this part of my voyage of mercy one of the great stabilising influences was the doctrine and experience of adoption. Mark Stibbe's book *From Orphans to Heirs* was the most impacting of a number of books on this topic.

Stibbe identifies that both John Wesley and Charles Spurgeon placed great emphasis on the Spirit of Adoption[2]. They recognised this doctrine might not appear to be very important at first sight. Stibbe writes:

...all new converts in the revival should not only be justified by faith, but also made aware of their adoption by the Spirit of God. If they only remained aware of their justification, then there was always a danger that they would enjoy a master relationship with God.[3]

Stibbe has clear, concise insight and answers for people who find themselves dealing with rejection, fear, legalism, unforgiveness, shame and addictions including to work and approval. He writes clearly that there is Spirit given revelation that moves us from

IF WE WANT TO LIVE AS SONS, WE MUST LIVE LIKE THE SON.

the faith of a slave to the faith of a son. If we want to live as sons, we must live like the Son. That is, we truly know the Father's acceptance; we are sustained by His acceptance, embracing intimacy. Our self worth and significance come from the initiative of the Father and the price He paid for relationship with us. We achieve or perform because we know we have work we can do by being Spirit led, not flesh driven.

Personally, I realised my adoption positioned me as a friend of God. John 15:15 states:

No longer do I call you slaves, for the slave does not know what his master is doing; but I have called you friends, for all things that I have heard from My Father I have made known to you.

I began to see that slaves do things for the master. They manage what they do and implement principles, practices and procedures. Friends, on the other hand, do things with one another. They nurture their relationship and love the ones they work with. I was now embracing a lifestyle of being with Jesus not just doing things for Him. My questions around church life changed from "What are we trying to do for God?" to "What does God want to do with and through us?" My change of focus meant church services were no longer predominantly a performance; rather they became a place of meeting together with God and one another.

As Stibbe reflects:

From now on, our sense of significance derives not from our performance but our position in Christ. Who we are, and indeed what we are, derives from the fact that we are adopted by grace. No longer are we preoccupied with the way others see us. We are wholly taken up with the way the Father sees us. No longer are we seeking the approval of others, we seek a deeper revelation of the Father's exquisite perspective of us. When the devil tries to exasperate us with what was true about our old self, we respond by reasserting the truth about our new self."[4]

Now I am convinced that His worth has made me worthy. Yet, it was not always this way. It is time to see how the lie was deconstructed and how the truth found somewhere to take root so that my thinking could be irrevocably changed.

MY TESTIMONY

*What lies behind us and what lies before us
are tiny matters compared to what lies within us.*

RALPH WALDO EMERSON

MY TESTIMONY

As I write, it is June 2006. While the threads and core of the fears and insecurities I will detail came into being many, many years ago, the process of unravelling it all became intense around November 2004. By February 2005, I was heading into a dark tunnel. Miraculously I was back out in the light around July 2005. It is now 12 months since then, and how different the world looks!

Rather than present the reader with unnecessary detail, I will try to stay with the main issues. Before 2005 I had head knowledge about the truths contained in Chapters Two to Five of this book. However, the reality of the truths presented in these chapters was birthed in my life through the tumultuous first six months of 2005. The process of establishing and consolidating these truths continues to this day.

In what follows there are five emails that I wrote on March 21 and 29, May 3 and 18 and June 27, 2005. They appear unamended to help the reader appreciate this stage of my voyage of mercy. I will be forever grateful to those who received these emails and carried me through this time in prayer and genuine love and acceptance. Without them the story would not have had the same ending. Again, I thank you all.

By November 2004 I had been the founding and senior minister of Christian City Church Whitehorse for 15 years. I was 48 years old and had been a Christian for nearly 23 years. Within the context of the Australian Christian community I led a church that was in the top two percentile by size and my name was relatively well known. However, in my secret inner kingdom, all was not well.

I could see at least 20 years of working life ahead of me. They were meant to be the best years of my life. I had figured out that by 50 years of age I should have learned enough from my mistakes to be useful and still have the energy and health to do something valuable through to at least

70. However, I was genuinely questioning whether my leadership skills had peaked and my personal shortcomings were such that I should hand the church over to someone else. I was no longer interested in building and maintaining an organisation for its own sake. I could see my own limitations were beginning to stifle the life of the church. I was also desperately aware of how far I had moved away from pursuing the supernatural origins of my Christian heritage. I had settled for a well organised and structured church that looked good but lacked the evidence of both my early Christian experience and that of the New Testament church.

> **I WAS NO LONGER INTERESTED IN BUILDING AND MAINTAINING AN ORGANISATION FOR ITS OWN SAKE.**

It was at this time that the possibility of another leadership role in a large non-government agency came to my attention. Lyn and I were on two weeks annual leave in January 2005 and the question of whether to stay at CCCW or apply for this other role was the centre of our conversation and prayer.

Towards the end of January 2005, I spoke with my friend and colleague Ian Jagelman seeking his advice and counsel. After patiently listening he said two things:

1. Making life changing decisions when in crisis was not the best thing to do (Lyn had already offered me this advice)

2. As a matter of highest priority I had to read *The Critical Journey*[1] by Janet Hagberg and Robert Guelich.

I chose to follow both pieces of advice. I also decided that I needed to trust my two senior associates and two board members with what was happening for me.

As I began to devour *The Critical Journey*, I reached Chapter Seven: *The Wall*. Over the next four days of reading in mid-February 2005 my world began to make sense. However, I also realised from what I was reading that I faced a clear choice of letting my life unravel as the way to move forward or to step back and sideways into a *safe* place where I knew I could live with and manage my fears.

Somewhere in the first half of 2004 I had come to realise that I was tormented by the fear of failure, the fear of rejection, the fear of being taken advantage of and the fear of being misunderstood. I knew these fears were there and I was learning to identify the sophisticated coping mechanisms I had developed to manage them. Now, in February 2005, it was obvious to me that the Lord was offering me a choice: live a life where I could manage these fears and appear to the rest of the world that I was still a contributor; or, confront these fears with Him, be free and see what He would then do.

The Introduction of *The Critical Journey* included comments like:

The Critical Journey is, at its core, a description of the individuals spiritual journey; our response to or faith in God with the resulting life changes... This book is about our journey, our ups and downs, our advances and retreats, our movement and our stuckness, our prodigal experiences as well as our self-righteousness, in response to what God is doing in our lives... The Critical Journey does not tell you exactly how or when to move along your spiritual journey. It does not offer any formulas for spiritual growth. But it does describe the various phases of our spiritual journey and illustrates how people act and think when in these places. It also describes transitions and crises that have caused others either to move or to get stuck at various stages...

Chapter one described some of the basic assumptions of *The Critical Journey* material:

For our purposes we have delineated seven stages on the journey of faith:

Stage 1	Recognition of God	God humbles us
Stage 2	Life of Discipleship	God grounds us
Stage 3	Productive Life	God rewards and exalts us
Stage 4	Journey Forward	God unsettles us
Stage 5	The Wall	God unmasks us
Stage 6	Journey Outward	God transforms us
Stage 7	Life of Love	God transcends us

We view the stages of faith as sequential and cumulative, rather than resulting in the label better... We do move around from stage to stage – back and forth... We can get stuck along the way; getting bogged down in an unhealthy way; a stage can become a cage...The journey of faith in our personal journey, and movement on the journey is the place of mystery and holy ground... God does not make us move. God's grace allows us to move... If we let the change or crisis touch us, if we live with it and embrace it as difficult as that is, we are more likely to grow and to move eventually to another stage or spiral in our journey. When we are most vulnerable, we have the best chance to learn and move along the way. In the midst of pain, there is promise..."

The material on stage five, *The Wall* is summarised by the following: *It is the place in which our wills meet God's will face to face and we are asked to relinquish our egos, our wounds and all else that stands between us and God... Its characteristics are:*

- *Knowing it is time to face the truth*

- *Letting God's will be our will*

- *Uncovering our deepest secrets, fears and wounds*

- *Considering unconditional love*

- *Feeling like we are in the muck...*

We felt very connected to God as long as things were under control or made sense. But now we find ourselves naked, defenceless and vulnerable so that we sense God's love and presence in a new way... Mystery lies at the core of the Wall, a mystery that ultimately defies explanation but includes discomfort, surrender, healing, awareness, forgiveness, acceptance, love, closeness to God, discernment, melting, solitude and reflection... The process involves finding out who we are, as opposed to who the world wants us to be... a sense of God's love for us in our humanness... it means embracing the frightened child..., the overachiever..., the insecure boy..., the risk taker... If we do not embrace these parts, they will dominate us... but embracing them we listen to what these qualities are telling us about ourselves... we emerge with a love for ourselves, for God and for others... Sometimes we feel so alone we think God has left us. Sitting alone in dark ambiguity is the result...

After reading *The Critical Journey* I knew two things. The first was that I wasn't going mad. Others had been here before me and others would follow. I was not alone or unique. The second was that the choice I already knew the Lord was offering me was going to lead to a 'dark night of the soul' if I chose to confront my deepest

...THE CHOICE I ALREADY KNEW THE LORD WAS OFFERING ME WAS GOING TO LEAD TO A 'DARK NIGHT OF THE SOUL'...

fears and deconstruct their attendant coping mechanisms. Knowing both these things made the choice a little easier.

At this point I brought Lyn, my two senior associates and two board members up to date with the material presented in *The Critical Journey*. I couldn't promise anything other than my commitment to whatever the process would bring to me. I asked for their prayer, their love and support and the space that I would need.

We simply cannot go through the Wall while working sixty hours a week, whether at home, or in an office, or on the road. We must set aside time for solitude – time to walk, to listen to God's voice, to think, to feel and to reflect.[2]

By mid February 2005 I had already been entrenched in the process surrounding the Wall for around nine months. I was genuinely wrestling with "who I was supposed to be and who the world wants me to be"[3]. I could see that my four fears, rejection, failure, being misunderstood, being taken advantage of, had come to life in my childhood. I had responded to the lies, hurts and wounds of growing up by believing that love, value and acceptance for me were inextricably tied to my performance. I was also aware that God was searching my inner secret kingdom with the purpose of having me exchange my fears and performance oriented mind-set for His love (1 John 4:18) and an acceptance oriented mind-set. I intuitively knew all this was necessary if I was going to live out my years serving Him with the power of the Holy Spirit. Compassion, love in action, is at the core of this life style. My self-serving, controlling, self-centred approach to managing my fears was a huge hindrance. I had to repent – change my way of thinking – so that my heart could be fully yielded to the will of God.

So, when I read the following reflections on the Wall I knew the next step in the process was to *embrace the frightened child...the overachiever... the insecure boy...the risk taker...(for) if we do not embrace these parts they will dominate us.*[4]

We don't necessarily get cured or erase our pain or become saints, but we learn to embrace our pain, how to stay with it and learn what it is trying to teach us, how to look fear in the face and keep moving into it. The Wall invites us each to heal ... The Wall clarifies for us whether we need to be different in the relationships, life, or work in which we are presently engaged... The Wall invites us to integrate our spiritual selves with the rest of us... We must face that which we fear the most... The Wall is the work of the heart but it is not for the weak of heart. That is why we have so many clever ways to avoid it... The Wall calls us to re-evaluate our image of God because in the Wall we encounter an endearing loving God... once this truth sinks in all else falls into place... To see how our personality was formed around our childhood experiences and our inherited traits, and to be aware of how we as adults, compensate or overcompensate for our childhood experiences... We are deeper, more compassionate, humbler, more aware of the pain of others and more loving on the other side of The Wall. It is an amazing gift – and quite a transformation for most of us. Our life is no longer our own. We are God's now...[5]

THE COPING MECHANISMS KEPT ME FROM FACING THE LIES, WOUNDS AND HURTS FROM WHICH I NEEDED TO BE HEALED AND SET FREE.

I had been dominated by the frightened child, the overachiever, the insecure boy and the risk taker. However, to embrace these parts of me I realised one thing would be essential. In the past I had not faced and embraced my fears, insecurities and these parts of me. Instead I had

107

developed sophisticated coping mechanisms to both avoid and deny their existence. These coping mechanisms of denial had become safety nets to stop me from falling into the recognition and reality of the truth. The coping mechanisms kept me from facing the lies, wounds and hurts from which I needed to be healed and set free. The only way to let the Lord reach the depths of my being and receive His answers was to no longer tolerate my coping mechanisms. The net result of this decision was that I started to fall into the abyss of my fears and insecurities with no way of coping other than depending on God and others.

My first two emails dated March 21 and 29 will help you see what was occurring:

March 21, 2005

Hi everyone.

I wanted to 'report in' in my progress through my wall. I need your prayers in particular. Your love and support are greatly appreciated as is keeping this information confidential. Thoughts, ideas and advice are okay as I look for the Holy Spirit to lead me into freedom.

I'm not sleeping particularly well. Not all that helpful!! There is plenty of pressure in my circumstances for my fears, insecurities and need to be in control to find expression in the old negative and *godless* ways. Four weeks ago we received notice that we need to vacate our current leased premises. Last week the tenants at the property we have purchased informed us that they will be leaving because of restrictions placed on them by council. Some key people have recently left the church 'under the Lord's direction' while others are just leaving. While new people are coming, the net result is negative growth. Not much is happening in the area of salvations. Our weekly giving is 'soft' and not enough to meet our projected budget.

While there are some great things happening, the above circumstances have the ability to cloud and infect my emotional well being. Not necessarily a bad thing, but it is draining and impacts my confidence. I wrestle with feeling like a liability (c.f. Jonah) but I do believe I'm still adding value and am still called to serve CCCW with my gifts in, and grace on my life (Let me know if you think otherwise).

A number of nights ago I woke up and was aware of the tap in our ensuite dripping. I got up and just closed the door of the ensuite. As I headed back to bed I felt the Holy Spirit talk to me. He said that my fears, insecurities and need to be in control were like the dripping tap. For the last 45 years they have slowly but methodically and completely influenced my thought life and emotional world. He showed me that I had used my gifts and strength of personality to close the door on the dripping and to pretend it wasn't really there.

I have become aware that one of the most significant ways I've managed my pain is to define myself according to 'success' measurement rather than who I am in Christ. However, the more insight I have, the more overwhelmed I am at how

> ...ONE OF THE MOST SIGNIFICANT WAYS I'VE MANAGED MY PAIN IS TO DEFINE MYSELF ACCORDING TO 'SUCCESS' MEASUREMENT RATHER THAN WHO I AM IN CHRIST.

pervasive all this stuff is in the way I interpret, interface with and move through my circumstances and relationships.

I don't want all the old points of reference to guide my sense of emotional well being and my thought life. I am gaining glimpses of revelation that help me however I still feel unnecessarily responsible and pressure to fix everything and/or make it happen. My emotional tank is low so while at times I cope, at other times I feel intimidated by my fears as I can't manage it anymore by 'closing the door'.

I'm so aware of when I feel rejected and that I'm failing – no doubt only in my own eyes. I've been so driven and I'm tired of being that way, yet I struggle to hold places of peace, joy and faith. I don't want to run the church organization, nor measure who I am based on what *it* achieves. I am meeting God in new ways and I want this to increase.

I hope this makes some sense. I hope it helps your prayer for me. I really know it will work out but I figure I have to let you right in to the present so that I can find the future.

Bye for now,

Love Peter.

March 29, 2005

Hi everyone.

Thank you for your continued love and support. I'm able to bring a good report. There has been a definite shift internally over the last week. It represents progress but not completion.

Over Tuesday, Wednesday and Thursday clarity came to me around some of my belief systems. This occurred through a range of circumstances but can be summarized as follows:

1. Deep down I don't feel accepted or valued and I use performance to compensate

2. I am limited in my capacity to fully enter into the richness of relationships because I have been unconsciously protecting myself particularly by being task focussed

110

3. I know people trust me, respect me and see me as responsible but I do not appreciate their genuine love for me nor fully realise the impact I make on their lives

4. I am not walking fully in who God has called me to be because I'm focussed on performance, task, getting things right, results etc. Unfortunately, to my embarrassment, the net result seems to be that I have not been abiding in my love for God. I try to count my blessings and yesterday's peak has become today's plateau and potentially tomorrow's gully

I set aside the better part of Friday and all day Saturday to seek God over these matters. The attached diagram may help to see what I was praying through and about *(See Appendix 1).*

As I prayed through these things I became aware of many thoughts including the following:

- I need God to create, not me to do

- If I can't do it I can't fail

- The future has to be built on Jesus

- Authority comes from intimacy

- I need to be set aside for the person of God

- I need a gift of revelation

- A dead man can't be rejected

- I can't keep going on the way I have to get here

Since Sunday morning I've been able to stay away from a whole way of thinking that inevitably took me into places of fear and my own effort. I have been able to more easily access my love for God and respond to my world from there. There is a joy that has returned, not fully blown, but none the less real.

On Monday I was reading Jack Frost's book Experiencing the Father's Embrace and these sections were insightful and helpful:

I HAVE BEEN ABLE TO MORE EASILY ACCESS MY LOVE FOR GOD AND RESPOND TO MY WORLD FROM THERE.

Page 80: *When we begin to serve God for the praise of man or to find identity in what we do, no matter how great the call of God is on our lives, no matter how powerful the gifts or the anointing flow in our ministry, that underlying attitude of self-love can begin to produce a hidden resentment and anger, fuelled by fear of rejection and a fear of failure. As soon as our service is no longer motivated by God's love but by a need to be needed or seen, we begin to drift away from the Father's heart of compassion and we will soon find ourselves in the older brother's shoes, slaving in the fields and thinking all along that we dwell in His house of love.*

Page 82: *...it is the unconditional acceptance of the Father that gives us our true value and self-worth. Deeply intimate relationships with other people are only possible between individuals who are secure in God's love, because the foundation of such relationships is love, trust and commitment. As soon as distance from God's unconditional love and insecurity begin to occur, intimacy with others becomes very difficult because we treat others in the way we feel about ourselves.*

Page 88-89: *Anticipate the homecoming your heavenly Father has planned for you. He understands your hidden core issues, your need for affirmation that may stem from your childhood. He sees the secret place in your heart that cries out for the unconditional love of a father, for the affirmation and affection that only He can provide.*

Thank you for continuing to walk with me. Any feedback will be gratefully received.

Love Peter

P.S. Please continue to treat this information as highly confidential.

So far so good. Then the wheels really fell off. My next email came five weeks later. The month of April was unbelievably painful. I allude to this in my email of May 3 but chose to stay on the up beat side for the sake of others. The reality though was that those closest to me knew how I wasn't coping particularly well. There were Sundays when I just couldn't go to church. I was so afraid that not enough people would be there for me to feel I was doing my job properly – unrealistic in hindsight but all too real in the moment. I was overwhelmed with the negative reality that I lived with. Thoroughly perplexed with how powerful my thought processes were in fearing the worst and astonished at how I had created a highly successful way of managing these inner tensions.

MY WORLD WAS BEING RULED BY NUMBERS AND DOING WHAT WAS RIGHT AS A RESPONSIBLE LEADER.

My world was being ruled by numbers and doing what was right as a responsible leader. My emotional well being was clearly and obviously impacted by: the number of people in church on Sunday; the amount of money in the offerings; the number of people who made decision to follow Jesus; the number of people being water baptised; the level of giving to the building fund; and too many other areas than I care to mention.

In and of themselves these numbers are fair and reasonable indicators. However, they don't exist in a vacuum. They represent standards that in most Christian's eyes represent something about success and failure. They are performance indicators. They are sought by denominational leaders, discussed amongst leaders across denominations, noted by congregants when they speak of their church and observed by outsiders when comments are being sought on matters that the wider community is interested in. They open doors into the lives of influential people because they in turn speak of influence.

Numbers make a difference in the way we are accepted, honoured and treated. This, in and of itself, is not necessarily bad (This a larger discussion than is the intent of this book). However, it can be the source of creating an environment where the fear and insecurity established and developed by the way we respond to failure in a performance based culture burst into flame in people's hearts. It did in mine.

Then there is the issue of doing what is right as a responsible leader. The only training I have for over half of what I do is from being on the job. Always learning on the run. As the organisation grows bigger there is more at stake. Some decisions have a very narrow margin of error.

The internal pressure around performance related issues is exacerbated by a range of factors birthed in how an individual handles the fears of poor performance. Taking things personally; not managing alternate points of view with good people skills; stifling healthy discussion because a conclusion may be agreed upon that you feel incapable of acting on; what will people think, say and do if this fails; getting your own way because you can't face being wrong; and many more. In a volunteer organisation like church, where trust is the currency for doing business, these issues present themselves regularly.

While these specific issues were not as great in my own world, my interactions with some church leaders indicated these issue were impacting their emotional well being. Could it be that my story is not an isolated incident? Is it possible that not only leaders but many Christians

COULD IT BE THAT MY STORY IS NOT AN ISOLATED INCIDENT?

in their day to day lives are struggling with performance based issues? If we are reflecting the community we are in, around matters of performance orientation rather than being a prophetic alternative, what are we to do about it?

There were numerous days when I felt detached from the realities around me. I lost some of my reference points for decision making and would either defer to the judgment of others or avoid involvement in the process of problem solving and decision making. There was an ever present strong undercurrent of hopelessness and despair. This was only mitigated by an undeniable awareness that God was right there with me. In the midst of all this, insights and revelation were providing a life line of hope that the path, although leading down, was actually leading me in the right direction. The next two e-mails dated May 3 and 18 will help you see this:

May 3, 2005

Hi everyone.

I've been meaning to write again for the last week or ten days. I can't believe that it's over a month since I've written. In that time I've had more good days than bad. I certainly feel like I'm continuing to make progress. However the bad days can be really bad. This is because I'm refusing to return to my old coping mechanisms when I experience fear and anxiety. Consequently there are no safety nets and I tend to plummet into some dark emotional places. The good news is that the only way out of there is to find God by standing on the promise that He's put in my heart to meditate on. So when I resurface, I actually come back stronger and more reliant on revelation knowledge. The net result is that my belief systems are starting to conform to the Word of God.

There are three main areas of insight that have occurred since I last wrote. Let me try to briefly unpack them for you.

1. I've realised that a significant way that I've managed my fear, anxiety and insecurity has been to play the roles that are expected of me. That is, I figure out what I think others expect of me, either as a son, student, pastor etc and then go about ensuring that my behaviour conforms to those expectations so that I experience 'success' and acceptance. A bit ugly really! Confronting sin can be a horrible experience.

> **CONFRONTING SIN CAN BE A HORRIBLE EXPERIENCE.**

Anyway, some of the consequences of living life this way are as follows:

- I tend not to connect deeply emotionally in life. I would keep people at arms length whilst appearing warm and affable. I've not really learned how to relax and be open in social settings. I tend to be more business like, somewhat mechanical and systematic in my relationships and certainly very performance aware.

- I've never really allowed myself to explore my passions and to find ways of expressing them. For example I always wanted to do history at school but mum convinced me to do geography. However I'm always asking questions about history but have never really taken the time to study it. This has recently changed. Another example would be that I've always had a fear of dancing. I've decided to see whether this is an expression of my sense of inadequacy and fear.

Therefore I'm going off to have dancing lessons with Lyn to see whether I do really like it or not.

- A question that I am exploring is "What's the best way for me to lead the church?" I've historically done what I think works for others and not necessarily understood how to be myself in the role.

- I have a great heart for the work that we as a church are doing in Cambodia but I also have a great heart for the life of the church that I am leading. I'm trying to understand what God is saying to me about my personal involvement in both. What's the context that the Lord is wanting me to express my leadership gift in?

2. Within some theories of psychology there is a proposition that fear comes from guilt. Recently as I was praying about this in my own life I had the blinding insight that I feel quite guilty about 'not being good enough'. I realise that my fears of rejection, failure, being misunderstood and being taken advantage of are all generated out of my pursuit to be good enough so that I then don't have to feel guilty.

In trying to be good enough I get caught in all sorts of behaviour that is either not Christ-like or dependent upon my own strength and not the Lord's. Some examples would be the role playing activity mentioned above, trying to make things right and get things right, the use of inappropriate emotional strength in trying to get my way, assessing life and particularly church through my fears and insecurities, and being somewhat self preoccupied with an unrealistic concern of how everything affects me. Someone please tell me I'm still a nice person!!

3. As I continue to face all the above I realise that God's love is transformational when it's received in vulnerability. I recognise that I need to allow myself to be loved

...GOD'S LOVE IS TRANSFORMATIONAL WHEN IT'S RECEIVED IN VULNERABILITY.

unconditionally by God even though I'm wretched, naked, and poor and feeling somewhat vulnerable. Ephesians 3:16-19 tells me that God's love is beyond knowledge. It seems to me that it's beyond just believing. The revelation of God's love comes by lingering long enough in His word to allow it to penetrate my woundedness.

So, in conclusion, it's fair to say that it's not unusual for me to feel emotionally jumbled up and somewhat disorientated. It seems that my greatest weakness at present is trying to adequately assess the impact all of this is having on the life of the church. I can only assume that it must bring some sort of restriction to what God can achieve amongst us. I can feel a little guilty about continuing to lead whilst not being particularly well emotionally. However, I can see the other side of the coin being that there is no-one else who could be doing better than I am. I can also see that if I can make it through here the future will be much brighter; not only for myself, but for those I am leading. In the meantime I don't really know how to interpret the facts about church life that are before me. I think I need to stop asking the question as to whether I'm doing good enough to continue walking in the privilege of leading this great congregation and let others guide and talk to me about my future as the Senior Minister of this church. It's not that I want to change the status quo but I feel incompetent for being able to know whether this would be best. I'm just going to have to trust that those who love me will let me know if and when that day comes.

I hope this all helps your prayers for me. I must admit I'm feeling pretty blooming vulnerable.

Regards, Peter.

May 18, 2005

Hi everyone.

Over the last week I've been in Newcastle speaking at a conference and church as well as doing a Pastor's Retreat with Lyn. During this time I've gained further insight which is summarized in the attached diagram. (I've tried to make it as understandable as possible.) *(See Appendix 2)*

My prayer life is currently directed at getting off the island of being good enough (and its associated guilt) and onto the land of God's grace where I am utterly dependent on His willingness to give Himself to me. I often feel like I am rowing away from my island of 'being good enough' to a land where I trust God deeply, love Him more fully and live by following a person not a map of principles and process i.e. walking in the Spirit. However, there are moments when a strong undercurrent of fear induced by my perception or circumstances temporarily sweeps me back towards walking in the flesh. At these times I feel:

a. That whilst I am turning a corner, the church is still labouring under the influences I have allowed and introduced from the way I have walked in the flesh

b. Guilty, ashamed and regretful because I now realize and see clearly how I have been leading and from where; and,

c. At times confused and uncertain about my future realising that it will not be until the end of 2005 that I will be in a good position to know God's will, yet in the present being increasingly aware of what has been motivating me and trying to understand the impact of what my passions are.

Please continue to pray for me and offer any insight you want. Thanks for being my friends on the journey.

Love Peter.

Six weeks then pass before I write again. I do recall that there were some bad days in this time. As I look back April and May always seem the darkest times. By June 27 (the date of the fifth email) I had begun to see clearly what had been and what I needed to reflect on and start to remain in. My performance oriented mind-set was starkly exposed for what it was. Janet Hagberg and Robert Guelich had been right when they wrote:

If we can ask of each perplexing or painful experience: 'What are you here to teach me?' then God will transform not only our inner world but eventually our outer world as well... If we can keep our eyes on God during the process – stay grounded in our healing experience, we will feel what the writers of the deep inner life call loving detachment or active indifference.

As you read the final email dated June 27 this should be apparent.

June 27, 2005

Hi everyone.

Well, it seems that I may have turned the corner. Thank you for your love and support to date. Your prayer in particular continues to be significant in my progress. It is great to be experiencing a freedom that I have only heard others speak of. Let me tell you, "where I am up to".

The central piece of what follows is the recognition and realisation that my frame of reference for all of life has been fundamentally flawed and somewhat contrary to biblical truth. I can separate what I'm experiencing into three broad areas:

1. FROM/TO

My place of reference is moving:

a. From a focus on my performance to underline my identity and establish my acceptance; To a focus on my total acceptance by God, that establishes my identity and empowers my performance in destroying the works of the devil.

b. From measuring my progress by what I have, what I do and what others think about me; To measuring my progress by my capacity to love.

c. From looking to character development as primary, resulting in a focus on self and a stronger desire to not grieve the Holy Spirit; To Looking for the power of divine encounters (while allowing for character development) resulting in a focus on the Lord, what He accomplished for us and who we have become in Him and a stronger desire to not quench the Holy Spirit.

The net result of these movements is a desire for intimacy with God where the source of everything I do is my surrender to God's love. This requires that I give myself to utter dependence on God's willingness to give Himself to me. I am learning to abandon myself to God by giving up control of

THE NET RESULT OF THESE MOVEMENTS IS A DESIRE FOR INTIMACY WITH GOD WHERE THE SOURCE OF EVERYTHING I DO IS MY SURRENDER TO GOD'S LOVE.

what matters most to me. This involves not worrying, being anxious and no longer trying to fix everything. I am also learning to place my total confidence in God by trusting someone I can't manage but whom I know to be good and kind.

I'm making progress. I probably haven't arrived yet. I know what I need to leave behind but I am yet to walk fully and confidently in the revelation I am receiving. For so long I have sought to 'do something for the Lord' which has kept the focus on my effort and created reference points of progress that I have sought to influence. Now I'm seeing that I both need to and want to 'allow the Lord to do things through me'. This helps the focus on my friendship with Jesus because of what He has done, and will create reference points for progress in my relationship with Him. What I can see and what occurs in the course of a day can be some distance apart.

2. THE POWER OF AGREEMENT

It is only as I see my old frame of reference for what it was that I actually see and understand the range and depth of lies I have been agreeing with. I have covered many of the lies and wrong belief systems in previous 'how I am going' emails.

More lately I have seen the following:

a. A vow I made to myself to never let myself be ashamed after spelling exams in Year Five at school;

b. That I have learned to influence people's behaviour for my benefit in the belief that I could see what was best;

c. That I felt isolated in my family of origin with the result that I learned how to be controlling, performance oriented and competitive;

d. From the above there was an underlying lack of trusting myself and therefore difficulty in trusting others by letting them into my inner world.

My agreement with my fears, doubts and insecurities coupled with an over zealous commitment to integrity and character development have seen me relying on my own strength and not leaving room for God to be God. I feel like Martha who was corrected for her 'distracted' service. She took her eyes off Jesus, trying to be the host of a banquet when all along He wanted to be the host of a banquet He had prepared. In her place of distraction she:

a. Was worried, that is, afraid that that which is important to her was not going to happen;

b. Was angry; that is, God you don't care and now I'm going to try and get you to do what I want; and

c. Was really trying to make herself feel better and impress God through her dedication, commitment and responsibility to/for the task(s) at hand.

I want to learn to serve Jesus from the position Mary adopted, characterised by:

a. Being in His presence as a result of His mercy;

b. Listening with a hungry and thirsty heart.

Like Moses I want to be convinced that I am a man God goes with.

3. A BLANK WHITE PAGE

As my frame of reference for life is shifting so significantly I recognise the need to live with a blank white page when it comes to two things:

a. How do I lead?

b. What do I lead?

How I lead revolves around such things as:

- From a love for God's presence and focus on relationship *more than* from well organised programs and successes measured by what I have and do and what others think of me

- Agreeing that Jesus wants to manifest Himself to me so I want to grow in my willingness to obey whatever He says

- My mind becoming a servant of the Spirit and being moved by compassion from intimacy

- Jesus being my model for life including character and power

What I do revolves around such things as:

- Do I keep leading CCCW? (My unequivocal answer is yes)

- Of what CCCW is currently pursuing, has the Lord really called us to pursue? (Nothing needs to change without the Lord's direction)

- How does the Lord want me/us to spend my/our time? eg. devotional life, travel, focus on who and what?

- What are the implications for the way we do church life on Sundays and during the week?

In the meantime it is steady as she goes, staying focused on Jesus and moving forward together. We have a lot to celebrate and be thankful for.

My Testimony

God is good and His plans are for a great future. It all lies before us as we follow the Holy Spirit.

Feel free to let me know what you sense the Lord is saying.

Love Peter.

At the time of writing the emails I was obviously concerned about confidentiality. This is no longer necessary because I am such a different person today. Hopefully by bringing them to print they will help others in how their voyage of mercy is unfolding.

7

Journaling My Progress

True life is lived when tiny changes occur.

LEO TOLSTOY

As I headed through the remainder of 2005 I kept a journal. Some of the entries may help in seeing the way progress was made.

Wednesday, June 29, 2005

Yesterday I was very mildly troubled by my perception of what others may be thinking of me. While I felt that I had not done anything untoward I was wrestling within myself over their apparent response, or in one case, lack of response. My wrestling was translating into that internal voice that can be demanding and driven. Thoughts that begin in justification but desire resolution in my favour. Not a place of love. I can feel the defensive internal posture. The mind then moves to include relationships from the past that appear to be unresolved and they get swept up in the process.

Yesterday certainly wasn't as overwhelming and dominating as in the past but it was there.

Being with the Lord this morning was so refreshing. Again I could see so clearly my need for humility with the Holy Spirit. As I bowed low yesterday's internal struggles dissolved into a place of rest and peace. Maybe yesterday things were heightened due to an absence of quality time with the Lord.

Certainly there was pressure in the stuff of yesterday to think my way to the solutions more than setting my mind on the Spirit and allowing the mind of Christ in me to bring the answers.

Thursday, June 30, 2005

The vague, underlying yet pervasive sense that I am responsible for the church's growth, therefore, focus on what I do that is turned towards my own strength, energy and problem solving; concern about 'results' reflect on me and this was last night and early this morning's battleground.

Both were sharply less intense than previously. Yet there is disappointment that the battlegrounds still exist. Also concern that I have not made the progress imagined.

Friday, July 1, 2005

That the source of my living would be the love of God. Today has been better than the last three.

I cannot allow the devil to tempt/deceive me over God's identity: He is good all the time; or, My identity: I am His friend.

Saturday, July 2, 2005

To break free – forever – from a self focused frame of reference. That is, how things affect me, reflect on me, tell me about success, influence me to consider what I need to do. Somehow this is tied to needing to be validated – even though I already am by God's love for me. Habits and ingrained ways of thinking are powerful things.

Jesus dying for me – so that I don't have to – and welcoming me into His family is all the acceptance I need – if only I can accept it as truth and not simply a principle.

Then there is grace – living in it and from it. Unmerited favour. Empowering presence. Yet not substituting reliance on God's grace when I am expected to participate.

Learning that to walk with the Holy Spirit is like sailing – looking for the wind – setting the sails accordingly. Surrendering to mind-sets and emotions that both demand and long for validation beyond being accepted

> **THEN THERE IS GRACE – LIVING IN IT AND FROM IT. UNMERITED FAVOUR. EMPOWERING PRESENCE.**

by Jesus results in striving and driveness. These do not cause a sailing boat to move when it is calm nor do they cause it to move when the wind is blowing. You can't manage the wind nor can you manage God.

Relying on God's grace is looking for the wind knowing that I am accepted, validated and can rest in faith and peace. Without the clear foundation of knowing and experiencing God's love everything is built on sand.

Persistence, endurance and resilience were never meant to be substitutes for living in God's love. God's love was meant to be the source of all my living.

Tuesday, July 5, 2005

I am enjoying reading the gospel of Luke. I see so much now through the eyes of God's love for all of us. The desire the Lord has to be good and bring blessing is clearly motivated by His heart. Much more than principle and process although there is clearly a place to know the ways of the Holy Spirit.

I feel like there are more questions than answers. I feel like I am back in kindergarten and just fumbling my way around. There are still internal tensions, conflict and doubt but I seem to be able to not get caught by it and stuck in it. Sunday morning before church was tough. Some stuff around the office pushes buttons. However, overall progress is clear.

Wednesday, July 6, 2005

When praying today two predominant things were coming through. The first was to do with forgiveness and regrets. I have made so many mistakes. In my drivenness and self preoccupation I have not seen things clearly. The devil's weapon is blindness, God's tool is revelation. I have made many bad calls of judgment and decisions from a place of blindness. I have regret about the consequences of these actions. Yet in Hebrews 11 Sarah is spoken of as a woman of faith even though she laughed at the thought of being pregnant. She was forgiven and God's view of her was changed forever.

Lord, please help me to 'not look back' and to see myself as you see me. A man God goes with.

The second thing was a deep awareness of the presence of the Holy Spirit. That He wants to be my friend and partner in life. That He will offer counsel and wisdom for every situation. That He will comfort my troubled soul and I don't need my old coping mechanisms. That He will help me – in every possible way.

Lord, please help me to turn to you. I want to avoid the response and reactions from perceived pressure. Help me to be humble and lowly, living from your love.

Sunday, July 10, 2005

Now it's Sunday afternoon. The first day of a 40 day fast – fruit, vegetables, eggs, cheese. Here we go... why, because I need to see more of God's power released through me, I need more revelation to remove the places of blindness in my heart. I seek more anointing to destroy the works of the evil one. I want to walk with the Holy Spirit into a future marked by God breaking into people's lives. I want to let God use me and work through me without the driving need to do something for God.

This morning I was able to approach church with much less anxiety and fear. I have made life so much about me that I

IT WAS GREAT TO GO TO CHURCH RELAXED. I WAS MUCH MORE OPEN TO WHAT GOD WAS GOING TO DO.

have suffocated in fear. My concern about things personally has resulted in controlling behaviour and thought life. But a new day is dawning.

It was great to go to church relaxed. I was much more open to what God was going to do. I will be preaching again tonight and I again am not agitated by getting it right. Bring this on more Lord.

Monday, July 11, 2005

Romans 12:3 (The Message)
The only accurate way to understand ourselves is by what God is and what he does for us.

Last night – in fact the whole day – at church yesterday was fantastic. The momentum continues. The key for me is to stay away from drawing from the results to meet my brokenness in the area of believing and experiencing that I am loved.

Yesterday was something God Did for us. We brought our obedience to the table.

Wednesday, July 13, 2005

Performance → Identity → Acceptance
Acceptance → Identity → Performance

When I ponder these two equations it helps me to fight and overcome the habitual internal pressure to measure and defend myself in and through life's circumstances. For example, yesterday there was pressure around our decision to start a new campus. The habitual response was to become emotionally agitated because I perceived that my performance in this matter was being questioned when I believe I have done all that was necessary. This resulted in my mind being set on defence not the

Spirit. This makes going to the fruit of the Spirit very difficult e.g love and patience.

While it is probably fair to say that my performance is being questioned and challenged when I live from the posture of acceptance by God – His love, belief and acceptance for/of/in me – then my emotional response is "oh well" and I can find the space to set my mind on the Spirit and then access the fruit of love, patience, kindness, goodness, self control etc.

This is very critical when I am needing to break from natural things to give birth to spiritual things.

Thursday, July 14, 2005

I'm beginning to realise that so much of what I study, what I think about, what I give myself to is designed to enhance my performance – not good!!

Today I reflected on my salvation, baptism in the Holy Spirit and early experiences of deliverance – it had nothing to do with my performance. These things occurred because they were in the heart of God and a reflection of what He does.

A mind-set that begins with acceptance results in performance on the basis of who God is and what is in His heart.

Saturday, July 16, 2005

I am at peace like I have not been before. I feel light and easy like I have not been before. I look at church and feel a trust in God's purpose that has not been there before. The need to ensure performance through control,

THE NEED TO ENSURE PERFORMANCE THROUGH CONTROL, THINKING AND PLANNING HAD GONE.

thinking and planning has gone. I am comfortable with being fluid and seeing what the Lord will do.

I really feel like I can float; place my total confidence in someone I cannot manage; let go control of what matters most to me; live from a place where love and my surrender to it is central; act our of acceptance not performance.

Sunday, July 17, 2005

Today was the first time in the last nearly 16 years that I woke and went to church on a Sunday free of anxiety and worry. I didn't feel responsible for the outcomes. However, I came away thankful for two healthy, strong meetings but disappointed there was not more evidence of the supernatural. This disappointment moved me toward both introspection about whether there is more I could be doing and examination of what others did looking for improvement. Both the introspection and examination led me away from peace, trust, rest, light and easy and into my own understanding and strength.

Being thankful and crying out in faith are the positions I found my way back to. Thankful for the strength that was not present even three months ago – strength of anointing, health, commitment, joy. Faith to look from God's perspective.

Wednesday, July 20, 2005

There is a growing sense of clarity and certainty about who I am, who God is and what I need to do. There is also a growing awareness that God is not only in control but preparing to do something beyond all I could ask and think.

I have spent my life working hard for affection and meaning. I have created purpose to serve my own need and meet my own pain. I have been purpose driven but from a motive for self-pleasure/ gratification/ fulfilment/ contentment.

I am beginning to see – revelation – that: knowing and loving God is our greatest privilege, being known and loved is God's greatest pleasure, knowing that I am loved by God is my gateway to freedom.

I finally get it... Relationship is a matter of the heart not principle and working for a response. That is, if I do this and this and this, then God/ they will do this. No... God already accepts me and wants me to accept Him for who he is – not what He has done or will do. That is, to know Him beyond what He does/ has done.

My life needs to be built from revelation and with anointing not from hard work and with principles.

Friday, July 22, 2005

I'm pretty weary now as it is day 13 in my fruit and veggie fast. Weary can result in irritable.

I so desire to stay focused on the matters of the Spirit so much more than the matters of the church and its growth. I want to be continually aware of the work and place of the Holy Spirit. For example, salvation is not for church growth and looking like we are succeeding – an unfortunate mind-set of my self centred past. No... salvation is a work of the Holy Spirit because God loves people – they are spiritually transformed when born again – Jesus wants this for all.

I am concerned to abandon my self serving perspective on life. As I'm fasting I find many moments in each day where I am profoundly aware of God, His love and His desire to touch other people's lives.

I'M LEARNING TO BE IN THE SPIRIT AND LOOK AT PEOPLE AND CIRCUMSTANCES FROM A HEAVENLY PERSPECTIVE.

I'm learning to be in the Spirit and look at people and circumstances from a heavenly perspective. My priorities are changing. My responses are more measured and based in the fruit of the Holy Spirit.

Sunday, July 24, 2005

The devil's job includes being the accuser of the brethren. This morning I woke up with the dull but penetrating feeling that I was a failure. There was a connection being drawn to my failure being represented in how church would be today – atmosphere, numbers in attendance, numbers saved.

Yet there was a loud, ringing and patient voice declaring that the answers are found in Jesus not in myself, that what I have been called to is impossible in my own strength. Jesus could not do it in His own strength. He only did what He saw the Father doing and said what the Father was saying. To try in my own strength would be vain. To be afraid of failure is conceited because it is saying I am totally responsible.

The fear of failure only drives me to:

- Worry – not believing that the Lord is and has the answer

- Control – but to be abandoned I want to give up control of what matters most to me.

- My Strength – but I am placing my trust in someone I can't manage.

Jesus role is to build the church. God causes the growth. My role is to be intimate with God. To declare the message of God's love which is why salvation, healing, and deliverance are available and possible.

My intimacy starts from being accepted. The revelation that I am chosen and adopted as a son. That the Lord has taken the initiative in everything.

I will trust you Lord because You are... and You don't expect me to do anything else than trust You.

Monday, August 1, 2005

Here I am today realising what an incredible journey I am on. The light that is being shone into the recesses of my mind is exposing just how carnal and performance oriented I have been. The mind is such a powerful force and I have trained the sentinels of my left brain so well to defend it with logic, reason and self centred protection.

My heart wants to lead me to places my mind will never go on its own. The right side of my brain and my heart are seeking places of initiative, creative response that will allow God to work through me. I have been so focused on what I do for God that I have lost sight of God working through me. Effort and striving have nullified the place of anointing and ultimately revelation.

Tuesday, August 2, 2005

I desire above all else to break from the natural things that are holding me back – performance, my own strength, striving, fear, trusting my mind more than my heart, the need to have everything organised.

I realise that I need to find a place of desiring the spiritual things because of my love for God and my love for others. *Not* because I need appreciation or to define myself on the basis of results. The devil will fight my progress in this regard. Temptation is not defeat, nor is it going backwards. The accuser of the brethren will try and drag me onto ground that is self-centred, defensive, fearful. The Holy Spirit is calling me to the ground of faith, hope and love.

Wednesday, August 3, 2005

My body is lacking so much energy with the fasting. I feel lethargic and have difficulty engaging my brain. Yet there's such a growing awareness of the Father's love. There is deep certainty that He will guide and lead us into the future. It is becoming crystal clear to me that without the powerful working of the Holy Spirit we are just playing games. There is a spiritual battle that we need to enter for the souls of people, their healing and deliverance.

> **THERE IS DEEP CERTAINTY THAT HE WILL GUIDE AND LEAD US INTO THE FUTURE.**

The truth though is that only God Himself can bring this to pass. I am hungry for God and His anointing like I have not been before. However, I can only exercise faith, live with hope and act out of love- the rest is up to my Lord. I know He wants it but it is His to give.

Friday, August 5, 2005

Just back from praying. There seems to have been a shift on the inside of me. It seems to me that I/we (family/church) are standing on the brink of some significant breakthrough. I am strangely at peace. Genuinely focused on love for God and others. Able to contemplate situations that could occur and find myself responding from other places. Places of rest that are not driven by what it means – either for myself or...!!

Saturday, August 6, 2005

Today I am very peaceful. I am thoroughly confident that God is in control .I genuinely accept that what I am endeavouring to do with my life is impossible without God. I do not feel compelled to try anymore.

It seems that I have genuinely accepted that what matters most is love. As I think about and consider tomorrow – Sunday and preaching – it is not surrounded with the need to perform and preach well. Rather I am centred on the reality that God loves, he wants to help me and others, so He will be there to minister life to all who are able to or choose to attend. I am operating out of a new space and framework. It is relaxed and focused on God and others, not me. It is a place of enjoying what each moment brings not feeling responsible for each moment.

Sunday, August 7, 2005

Here I go – back into the fray. After four weeks out of the office and away on Sundays, today I was preaching in both morning services. It really felt different. I found myself operating out of a different space. Yet, after it was all over – and it went really well – I found myself tempted to head back towards the observations and assessments that have historically trapped me in my own strength. I really hope this is the power of old habits. They take awhile to die!

YET I KNOW THAT THE OLD SPACE HASN'T BEEN WORKING.

I can so clearly see where I want to live from, yet it feels a little awkward, unfamiliar, untested and unproven. Yet I know that the old space hasn't been working. I haven't broken from the *natural* place/imperative of performance so I've given birth to lame things not spiritually dynamic things.

Tuesday, August 9, 2005

Monday came and went 7.30am to 10pm non stop. First day back in the office. Lot's of pressure. A builders quote that went up 25 percent ($560,000). A meeting with a council officer where it was clear they were not really going to help. The dawning reality that there would be a 2-3 month gap between leaving Bank Street and getting into Rooks Road. The need to coordinate everyone and our response to all the above. Then in the gaps of this roller coaster, there was admin, people and leaders meetings.

However... the incredible, great and wonderful thing was that I responded from the new place of knowing I am loved and accepted by God. I completely avoided the place of performance and the patterns of response that have been driven from there. I was not anxious, fearful, demanding, controlling, driven etc. Rather, there was genuine peace that God was in control and all was going to be well. What a powerful test of the truth that God has birthed in me.

Sunday, August 21, 2005

It is said that God cannot do a great work through us until He has done a great work in us. The great work being done in me this year is wonderful. Where it all goes now will be strongly influenced by the leading and empowering of the Holy Spirit.

Spiritual disciplines and charismatic experience both have their place in the believer's life. However, there are some things that only charismatic experience will achieve. It is the truth that my heart will lead me places my head will never go. When we try to achieve through spiritual disciplines what is accomplished by charismatic experience we become slaves to law.

Monday, August 22, 2005

Intimacy, acceptance, adoption as a son are all keys to living from the place of revelation that in Christ I (we) have access to all that the Father is. Luke 13:31, Psalm 119:91, Ephesians 1:3 all make it clear that everything is ours. So, the thing is how to access the parallel universe of heaven so that it invades earth. Not by works but by revelation and faith. God is good and wants to give life. I need to allow my mind to be renewed to the realities of heaven.

Wednesday, August 24, 2005

My dreams last night were centred around feelings of failure – from a young age and possible rejection is perceived from a young age. My prayer time this morning was grateful for the revelation of adoption but seeking further freedom and healing in my wounded soul. The internal push to control my world to escape the sense of failure and rejection is incredibly high and strong.

Monday, August 29, 2005

It has been an interesting 24 hours. Last night's church service was very ordinary (and disappointing). Today we (I) learned that Lyn and I had lost a significant amount of money in an overseas investment gone wrong – ouch!! Both good circumstances to test how free I really am of my performance base/orientation.

While I can recognise signs that I am still vulnerable to be negatively influenced I can report that it is minor. There was temptation, and probably just old ways of thinking, that wanted me to be fearful, controlling and concerned about what others would think. However, I was able to see it for what it is/was and not be drawn into it. A little flat but not overwhelmed or driven.

Thursday, September 22, 2005

This is a very real time of trusting God. There are so many things that are completely beyond me to achieve at present. As I pray about them answers seem to come although they are yet to fall into place as I am moving toward them. However, there is a real peace in my heart that all is well. I sense that not only is the Lord leading but I can fully trust where He is leading. There is no emotional pressure to make things happen or be driven. There is just great confidence that all will be well.

Saturday, September 24, 2005

The faith of a son or a slave has been running around inside of me today. Clearly I'm in transition.

The faith of a slave has led me to performance, guilt and management. The faith of a son leads to rest, peace, faith and surrender that begins to see that Father's will be done above all else. So being led by the Spirit takes on great importance and significance.

Wednesday, October 12, 2005

Being dependent and being led...

So many issues that are unresolved and being attacked seem to come unstuck or are thwarted. My hope has to be in the Lord. He is the Provider, Builder, Healer, Saviour, Deliverer.

Thursday, October 13, 2005

Yesterday was interesting!! I broke somewhat under the *perceived* pressure of financing Rooks Road. On Tuesday I recognised a level of despair around the levels of sickness and could sense some internal pressure around Rooks Road. I thought I was doing alright but I wasn't really, and it came spilling forth in my weekly meeting with Rudolph.

In 2 Corinthians 4 Paul identifies being perplexed but not despairing. I am perplexed by a range of things. However, I'm only just seeing that when I get perplexed I do a couple of things:

- I take responsibility for fixing it

- I take it a little personally

- I worry what others will think – this also feeds off what others have thought in the past

- I see issues through a winner/loser set of lenses which then results in the need to win my way rather than letting God sort it out

Tuesday, 18 October, 2005

I CAN BE FAILING BUT NOT BE A FAILURE.

I can be failing but not be a failure. If the context of my meaning is performance then when I fail, I am a failure. I take it personally. Defend myself and/or begin to strive for success. However, if the context of my meaning is acceptance then I can fail and not be a failure. In part it is only from this place that I can truly boast about my weakness so that God's power can be perfecting in them. It is from here that my interest is not in what it means for me but what it means for God and others.

Thursday, November 3, 2005

Hi Lord. I'm beginning to realize that warfare is just part of every deal. It doesn't speak of failure or being wrong or being inadequate. Rather, it speaks of the devil's character to rob, steal and destroy. He can't help himself adopting this position around everything we try to do. Therefore there will be struggling, false reports, disappointments, frustrations but they are not be believed - we walk by faith not by sight – and they certainly do not point to nor determine the outcome – we are overcomers through Christ Jesus.

Patience, rest, peace, trust, endurance are all weapons of warfare. They are attractive to God because this is how He responds. These are not passive or indifferent responses. Rather, they position us to truly take and walk in the authority we have in Jesus. They allow us to live in the Spirit and fight in the spirit realm.

Saturday, November 5, 2005

The clear message of the last two days is about trust. However, also recognising the way the devil works at deceiving the imagination to see outcomes that are not based in favour and blessing. The performance orientation of the past has always made it difficult to see the devil's work. Being self centred and avoiding failure because I took it personally gave credibility to an imagination steeped in problem solving and avoiding things in my own strength. When the beginning point is God's love and intimacy then acceptance creates a context for seeing the rob, steal

THE PERFORMANCE ORIENTATION OF THE PAST HAS ALWAYS MADE IT DIFFICULT TO SEE THE DEVIL'S WORK.

and destroy motive of an imagination that is contemplating the worst. Acceptance presupposes the best.

Friday, November 11, 2005

Boy, is it really nearly a week since I've written here? It is probably a good indication of how busy I am and how tired I am feeling. The busyness is just work related. Having our house on the market brings with it its own time demands and timetable restrictions.

Having acknowledged the challenge it is still true to say that my inner world is healthy and prospering. I sense both the peace of God and the leading of the Holy Spirit. It is not difficult to stay in a strong place of trust in the midst of a lot going on. If I do stumble in trust I find my way back quickly.

I am enjoying all that is going on. I see the Lord bringing things to me to have the vision and dream progress. I find greater levels of patience and a capacity to make room for things to happen. I certainly don't know where a number of things are going. I know all is well but how to get to certain places is not clear. I am greatly encouraged by what I hear other saying the Lord is doing in their lives.

I know that I am the most ready I have ever been to lead but I feel the most inadequate at the same time. I'm way in over my head...

In December 2005 I was able to represent my insights and what had been revealed to me in the following way:

PARADIGM OF ACCEPTANCE	PARADIGM OF PERFORMANCE
Work FROM love	**Work FOR love**
• HIS business:	• MY business:
• What is HE saying and doing	• Being in control
• Faith & obedience	• Avoiding fear
• Concern for signs & wonders	• Concern for reputation
• Whose presence matters	• Who is present
• How do I get to enter God/s world	• How do I get God to enter my world
What's FIRST for HIM:	**What's FIRST for ME:**
• Being	• Doing
• Obedience	• Being right
• Vulnerable & weak	• Gifts & abilities
• Grace	• Activity
My FOCUS is on/ I care ABOUT:	**My FOCUS is on/I CARE about:**
• His MAJESTY	• Outcomes
• His power	• Opinions
• His promises	• Self
• His life	• Safety
Outcomes:	**Outcomes:**
• God's love defined by revelation	• God's love defined by circumstances
• Faith in nature & character of God	• Sight is activated over faith

The consolidation of the truths presented elsewhere in this book was vital for my own personal experience of freedom but also for the benefit it will bring to others, in particular those I lead. Joseph's personal victories and ultimate belief that God would fulfil the dreams of his life, caused Joseph to become a corporate blessing that protected all those who came under him (Genesis 31-48). Similarly, David's victory over Goliath became a corporate blessing as all Israel lived in peace because of it. If David had died all Israel would have served the Philistines. Leaders need to understand that because we *individually are members of one another* (Ephesians 4:16) our actions and attitudes have consequences that are magnified many times over.

Here are the observations of those closest to me regarding the impact of my change on the life of the church I lead:

WAYNE BACK (EXECUTIVE PASTOR)

I find Peter to be more willing to let people use authority along with the responsibility they have been given and willing to let them take care of the detail. I think that people are taking up greater ownership for their departments and for the church as a whole and leaders are rising to new places of fruitfulness with their increased authority and passion. There is certainly a much greater desire for the things of the Spirit as well as genuine love for one another amongst the church members. The church has also been transformed in its attitudes to new people. Once we would have been described as unfriendly, but the majority of new people now report us to be very welcoming.

ANDEE SELLMAN (CHURCH BUSINESS LEADER)

I can see from the outside that Peter is allowing leaders around him to develop their own way of doing things even though it is very different from his own style. Primarily I see Christian City Church Whitehorse as being built on relationship rather than task. Peter has actually been able to walk this quite well as I look in from the outside. I can see that the Holy Spirit is able to have much greater access to affect the life of the church. There is no doubt that the worship has much more freedom and the worship team has been encouraged to wait and see what the Lord might be wanting to do rather than rushing on and getting finished. I believe that Peter has given this freedom and as a result we see the moving of the Holy Spirit in a greater and deeper way.

HILARY BACK (STAFF MEMBER)

The thing most noticeable to me was the changes in key leadership and then that leadership being able to move into a whole new place because of the changed atmosphere around them and the church of liberty and freedom.

HANNAH EASTON (OUR ELDEST DAUGHTER)

The emphasis is definitely on relationship, not task, and we staff, leaders and congregational members have been released into greater levels of freedom. Whilst there are still great levels of vision and direction Dad pours into the church, there is no longer vision, direction and a set of plans of how we are going to get there. There is vision, direction and a desire to enjoy the journey of how God walks with us and how we walk with each other to get to the places He has for us.

I certainly believe that if you hadn't agreed to go on a journey *with* God into the issues, fears and insecurities you describe, we wouldn't be where we are today as a church. Your willingness to go on the journey has led all of us into grater levels of freedom.

RICK PORTER & GEORGE NEOPHYTOU (MEMBERS OF THE EXECUTIVE LEADERSHIP TEAM)

Having seen Peter come though a painful and difficult period it has been a joy to see a change in Peter's leadership approach. Peter, as Chairman of the ELT, was always quite agenda and outcome focused, quite normal for that role, but now he is speaking about things like
— Relaxation of office policy
— Succession planning and generational planning
— The realization he works with God and not for God and that he needed his staff to understand that they too, in turn, work with him – not for him.

The ELT meeting agenda is no longer the driver of the meeting, it's a bit more like 'What does God want us to achieve out of this gathering?', and at times, the agenda has barely gets a look in. We have also observed less 'personal input' into planning, vision and agenda and a visible desire to see others around him contribute.

It is most definitely a different Peter we work with today than it was 12 months ago. Although we have the same level of confidence in him today and are as sure of his willingness to follow the Lord and submit himself to Him now as we had then we do believe that together we are now positioned for the quantum leap forward we have been expecting.

The way I now live the Christian life is profoundly different. Over the last two years I have not only learned a lot about myself. I believe that I have seen the necessity of making sure that second things do not become first things. Order is important when it comes to the way we follow Jesus and serve Him and others. When the order is right then we are thinking as God thinks.

Romans 12:2 states:

And do not be conformed to this world, but be transformed by the renewing of your mind, that you may prove what the will of God is, that which is good and acceptable and perfect.

For God's will to be done on earth, for His kingdom to be established in the lives of many, for the realities of heaven to be the daily experience of people we must place the emphasis where God places it. Bill Johnson[1] is right when he says:

Our assignment has never been about what we can do for God, but what can God do through us...We must repent and renew our minds...The only way to consistently do Kingdom works is to view reality from God's perspective...The mind is the essential tool in bringing Kingdom reality to the problems and crisis people face. God has made it to be the gatekeeper of the supernatural...The renewed mind, then, reflects the reality of another world...Only a renewed mind can consistently bring Kingdom reality to earth...Every thought and action in your life speaks of allegiance to God or to satan. Both are empowered by your agreement... 'Re' means to go back. 'Pent' is like the penthouse, the top floor of a building. Re-pent, then, means to go back to God's perspective on reality... He wants you to see reality from God's perspective, to learn to live from His world toward the visible world... Most Christians have repented enough to be forgiven, but not enough to see the Kingdom... The idea of Kingdom power and spiritual conflict unsettles some people, but without power, the gospel is not good news. Jesus never made the gospel simply a doctrinal exercise... In the New Testament, the very word for salvation means healing, deliverance, and forgiveness of sin... He did miracles as man in right relationship with God because He was setting forth a model for us, something for us to follow... That is the nature of our call – it requires more than we are capable of... Jesus lived in constant confrontation and conflict with the world around Him, because Kingdom logic goes against carnal logic... How is your life contradicting the way life works for most people in your city?... A renewed mind sees the way God sees. It receives His impressions and becomes a creative force to release His expression of dominion on planet Earth...

BEFORE
BUT NOT
WITHOUT

8

It is within my power either to serve God or not to serve Him. Serving Him,
I add to my own good and the good of the whole world. Not serving Him,
I forfeit my own good and deprive the world of that good.

LEO TOLSTOY

THE IDEA EXPLAINED

The application of truth is influenced by order, emphasis and context. Order is a significant key in the way truth is to be viewed. As outlined in previous chapters many of life's paradoxes require that we live with a *both/and* approach not *either/or*. Some people are predominantly black and white in their views of every aspect of life and think in boxes. Those who are comfortable to live with grey and more uncertainty are able to think outside those boxes. Put another way, they move up and down a range of opinions about a subject, a ladder if you will, and do not have to accept one rung of the ladder as the only acceptable view. There are certain absolutes even for those who live with grey. For example: Jesus, the Son of God, born of a virgin, shed His blood for the forgiveness of sin and is the only way to God. Matthew 23:23 records Jesus saying:

"Woe to you, scribes and Pharisees, hypocrites! For you tithe mint, dill and cumin, and have neglected the weightier provisions of the law; justice, mercy and faithfulness; but these are the things you should have done without neglecting the others."

The Pharisees emphasis was distorted. Love and justice were mixed up because their motivation appears to have been more about control than free will. In Luke 4:3-12, even the devil uses Scripture to try to persuade Jesus of his point of view. However, the devil uses Scripture out of context and so perverts its truth. Order, emphasis and context are important in understanding the application of truth. When we get the cart before the horse we are not going to make any progress at all.

C.S. Lewis in one of his many essays tackles the topic of first and second things. Lewis observes that:

every preference of a small good to a great good, or partial good to a total good, involves the loss of the small or partial good for which the sacrifice is

157

made1. He then expands on this law, as he calls it, by concluding: *You can't get second things by putting them first; you can get second things only by putting first things first.* Lewis illustrates this point by observing: *The man who makes alcohol his chief good loses not only his job but his palate and all power of enjoying the earlier...levels of intoxication.* He then proposes that the logical question is: "What things are first?" He goes on to explore his question in the context of how to make civilization safe. He concludes,

To be sure, if it were true that civilization will never be safe until it is part second, that immediately raises the question, second to what? What is the first thing? The only reply I can offer here is that if we do not know, then the first and only true practical thing is to set about finding out.

Kris Vallotton makes the observation that: "Whenever truth is out of order it creates disorder. Perversion is *the wrong version*"2. Just as words need to be in order to qualify as truth so do ideas. For example, it is one thing to say: "My dog is a girl". It is another thing to say "My girl is a dog".

My voyage of mercy has resulted in a conviction that to live the fullest Christian life available we need to follow a range of Biblical principles

THERE ARE FIRST AND SECOND THINGS IN THE WAY SOME DIMENSIONS OF BIBLICAL TRUTH ARE APPLIED.

that declare that you can't get second things if you put these second things first. Equally though, you can't get first things in the absence of second things. For example, drawing on the previous chapters it is clear that it is acceptance before performance, but not without performance. Alternatively Placing performance before acceptance, even if it is not without acceptance, results in disorder and perversion in the life of every believer who lives this way. There are first and second things in the way some dimensions of Biblical truth are applied. This is well declared in 1 Corinthians 13:13, But now faith, hope, love abide these three; but the greatest of these three is love.

ACCEPTANCE BEFORE PERFORMANCE BUT NOT WITHOUT PERFORMANCE

God wants friends, not slaves.

A performance based mind-set with its attendant fears and insecurities leaves us feeling that God wants more from us. Without a revelation of adoption and its associated acceptance, the performance based areas in our lives will be capitalised on by the evil one and we will be slaves again to fear. There is a transition to be made from slave to friend. John 15:14-15 declares:

"You are My friends if you do what I command you. No longer do I call you slaves, for the slave does not know what it is his master is doing; but I have called you friends, for all things that I have heard from My Father I have made known to you."

Slaves obey out of fear, no matter its origins or point of influence. Friends obey out of love, a heart that is willing to dare to believe that God is at work through them. Slaves live at **SLAVES OBEY OUT OF FEAR... FRIENDS OBEY OUT OF LOVE...** the extremities of the master's affections, whereas friends are up close and personal, privy to not only knowledge but also heart motivation and reasons for activity.

When performance comes before acceptance we read and view Scripture through a slave's mentality. The idea of friendship is attractive and we may even try to get there through self effort. However, our heart will struggle to embrace the fact that God is deeply interested in us, and our opinions, thoughts and feelings. Performance leads to a one dimensional view of what it means to have relationship with God. It overemphasizes obedience and underemphasizes friendship with the result that we are robotic, soldier like and plagued with uncertainty.

Abraham, Moses, Paul and others were friends of God. Jesus wants us to be friends. We can learn from these men some of the characteristics that mark friendship with God. They knew they were accepted by the Lord and their acceptance was not based on their performance. It was from this posture that Abraham questioned God, debating with Him on the basis of friendship (Genesis 18:23-25). Equally, Moses said to God 'You are more important to me than any vision that I have for my life' (Exodus 33:12-17). In other words, even at the risk of upsetting You, God, I want You more than I want what You do.

Again, Paul recognized that sometimes when God prophesies to us, He is looking more for interaction than He is for blind obedience (Acts 21:10-13). 1 Corinthians 13:4-8 describes the nature and character of God as it applies to us. For example, God does not seek His own and He takes no thought to Himself (1 Cor 13:5). That is, God is not selfish and He is not just hanging around with us so that He can get His own way. Kris Vallotton and Bill Johnson make the bold assertion that: *God often restrains His strength so that He can have relationship with His people.*[3]

As I have made the transition in my thought life from slave to friend by living with acceptance before performance, I have found a significant change in my motivations towards God. When it was performance before acceptance my questions to God were around, "What do You want me to do for You?" and, "What do I need You to do for me?" Now that it is acceptance before performance but not without performance, the questions are, *"What do You want to do WITH me?"* and, *"What do I want to do WITH You?"* The questions and motivation of a friend and slave are different.

I have made two observations.

It is possible for people to live from a position of acceptance alone. They disregard the role of performance in becoming fruitful for kingdom purposes. Their appetite for God is focused on encounters with Him for encouragement. They go from one anointed meeting to the next looking for an atmosphere that blesses them. They become a reservoir of blessing not a river of blessing. Our position needs to be acceptance before performance, but not without performance because we are also called to be fruitful and do good works (John 15, James 1). We are to be rivers of blessing to the communities we live in. We are not waiting to go to Heaven. We are pursuing a lifestyle where Heaven invades earth through us, a life style of friendship with God.

I have also noticed some people try to practice the principles of faith from a performance mind-set, leading only to disappointment. They endeavour to move God's hand by concerted praying and believing. Rather than striving to enter the rest of faith, they strive in self effort. Faith that releases God's world to ours is characterized by peace and rest. Our

RATHER THAN STRIVING TO ENTER THE REST OF FAITH, THEY STRIVE IN SELF EFFORT.

entrance to this place of peace and rest is often through standing firm during the process of transformation and in spiritual warfare against our enemies of fear, doubt, insecurity, scepticism, cynicism, unforgiveness and bitterness. Where there is a performance based mentality people can mistakenly strive both in warfare and transformation by praying more, fasting longer, confessing the word louder and so on. These disciplines can't hurt you, but they can lead to frustration and great disappointment because they are based in self effort. I have been overwhelmed at how powerful the doctrine of adoption is when I remain in it, and behold the God who initiated it. Its light defeats the accomplices of a performance based mentality every time. Then the peace and rest of faith are a daily reality from which to begin to see Heaven invade earth.

MERCY BEFORE JUDGMENT BUT NOT WITHOUT JUDGMENT

Mercy and judgment are clearly related to acceptance and performance. Judgment is such a pervasive characteristic of our culture that it warrants some consideration. We are all familiar with being judged. As toddlers our behaviour was judged and continues to be judged by others, no matter how old we are. We make judgments regularly about politicians, celebrities, the level of service provided. In fact, the media for all the benefits they bring constantly present extreme stories and report in such a way as to encourage us to make a judgment and take a position.

We will never escape judgment in life. In fact, judgment, in and of itself, does not have to be a negative thing. For example, leaders, innovators and inventors often judge the *status quo* as needing to be challenged and changed. The net result is progress and, in general, a better way of living or doing things. There are aspects of judgment that create negative outcomes in a performance based culture. Firstly, we are not capable of accurate judgment because we are not all knowing. Only God knows everything, so we do not have all the evidence at hand when we are making most judgments. Secondly, we often ascribe motive to others in our judgments when we are not able to read their hearts. These motives are generally negative in nature and cause us to think less of the other person. Thirdly, we are emotionally impacted, often not for the better, by being judged and being a judge of others. The emotional impact of judgment generally strips us of love in either receiving it or giving it.

Judgment is more prevalent than mercy. Like the older son in Luke 15:11-32, for the majority of people it is judgment before mercy. Yet, God is patently not like this. Religion portrays Him as a judge. We see Him as we are, and expect Him to be judgmental – with consequences!! We inherently believe He is interested in what is wrong when in truth He is far more interested in what is missing. We try to help bring holiness to the church and the world through *righteousness* judgment. Yet Scripture is as blunt as possible at this point, *Do not judge so that you will not be judged* (Matthew 7:1-5).

> **WE INHERENTLY BELIEVE HE IS INTERESTED IN WHAT IS WRONG WHEN IN TRUTH HE IS FAR MORE INTERESTED IS WHAT IS MISSING.**

God is love (1 John 4:8). Therefore, where the word love appears in 1 Corinthians 13:4-8 we can legitimately put the word *God*. We can know that God is patient and kind and does not take into account a wrong suffered. This is why Paul writes that 'the kindness of God leads to repentance' (Romans 2:4) not the anger, retribution or judgment of God. It is why Jesus could confidently say, *"...for I did not come to judge the world, but to save the world"* (John 12:47). One of the most stunning statements of the Bible that defies all religious thought and dispels one of the greatest attacks on God's character states, *For God has shut up all in disobedience SO THAT HE MAY SHOW MERCY TO ALL.* (Romans 11:32. Capitals are my emphasis). How big is that!!

God is motivated to show mercy and be merciful (James 2:13). He will do all that is possible within the tension of His unfathomable love and His supreme holiness to be merciful. His desire is for mercy to prevail before judgment but if we do not respond to mercy then judgment will come (Exodus 34:6-7).

Then the Lord passed by in front of him and proclaimed, The Lord, the Lord God, compassionate and gracious, slow to anger and abounding in loving kindness and truth; who keeps loving kindness for thousands, who forgives iniquity, transgression and sin; yet He will by no means leave the guilty unpunished, visiting the iniquity of fathers on the children and on the grandchildren to the third and fourth generations.

To be God's friend, to pray with confidence that He hears us, to minister to others who are broken, hurt and distressed having faith that God will respond, all this and more is dependent on mercy before judgment but not without judgment. This is why Jesus implores us to forgive (Matthew 6:14-15). The act of forgiveness places us in the seat of mercy and releases the very heart of God into that situation. For those who have put performance before acceptance and not the other way around, judgment before mercy is often both their experience and default position. It will diminish their relationship with God, others and themselves.

PRESENCE BEFORE PRESENTS
BUT NOT WITHOUT PRESENTS

Recently we had a series of meetings in our church with Bill Johnson. The meetings went over three days with a session in the morning and one in the evening. The Lord was healing many people and many others were being renewed in their faith and stirred by the Lord. Word had spread, and by the third night a good number of people were lined up outside before the doors opened. I was in the foyer talking with a staff member when the doors were opened. Those who had been waiting were now literally running full speed from both external entries toward the auditorium with no apparent concern for the safety of others – including my staff member and myself! I would love to one day report this same phenomenon and enthusiasm for the prayer meetings we conduct.

> **WE DISPLAY GREAT DESIRE FOR THE PRESENTS GOD HAS FOR US... BUT LESS DESIRE FOR HIS PRESENCE.**

My point is this. We display great desire for the *presents* God has for us – in this case healing and empowerment, but less desire for His *presence*. We more easily spectate than we do participate. Moses approached life with the Lord differently. Exodus 33:1-3 tells the following story:

Then the Lord spoke to Moses, "Depart, go up from here, you and the people whom you have brought up from the land of Egypt, to the land of which I swore to Abraham, Isaac, and Jacob, saying, 'To your descendants I will give it.' And I will send an angel before you and I will drive out the Canaanite, the Amorite, the Hittite, the Perizzite, the Hivite and the Jebusite. Go up to a land flowing with milk and honey; for I will not go up in your midst, because you are an obstinate people, lest I destroy you on the way."

Many of us would have said, "Wow, an angel that will ensure we get everything God has promised to give us. We get the Promised Land. Our prayers have been answered. All the 'presents' are going to be ours."

Not so Moses. Look at his response in Exodus 33:12-17 to the Lord's suggestion:

Then Moses said to the LORD, "See, You say to me, 'Bring up this people!' But You Yourself have not let me know whom You will send with me Moreover, You have said, 'I have known you by name, and you have also found favor in My sight.' "Now therefore, I pray You, if I have found favor in Your sight, let me know Your ways that I may know You, so that I may find favor in Your sight Consider too, that this nation is Your people." And He said, "My presence shall go with you, and I will give you rest." Then he said to Him, "If Your presence does not go with us, do not lead us up from here." "For how then can it be known that I have found favor in Your sight, I and Your people? Is it not by Your going with us, so that we, I and Your people, may be distinguished from all the other people who are upon the face of the earth?" The LORD said to Moses, "I will also do this thing of which you have spoken; for you have found favor in My sight and I have known you by name."

Moses honours his friendship with the Lord by saying, 'If You are not going, I'm not going either'. The presence of God was more important to Moses than the presents of God.

Jesus indicates the importance of this order in His words recorded in John 15:7, *"If you abide in Me, and My words abide in you, ask whatever you wish, and it will be done for you."* Jesus identifies for us that He, the living Word of God, is to be the source for our fruitfulness. Yet it is not just Him alone, but it is our relationship with Him. It is our pursuit of His company, our desire for His presence that is the key to our effort. The cry of the psalmist (Psalm 42:1-2) is to be our cry too:

As the deer pants for the water brooks, So my soul pants for Thee, O God. My soul thirsts for God, the living God; When shall I come and appear before God?

166

THE PRIZE IS TO KNOW HIM... TRUSTING THE ONE WHO INVADES THE IMPOSSIBLE WITH THE SUPERNATURAL.

The prize is to know Him. From this place we are stirred with compassion to build His kingdom with power and justice. We are not to reduce ministry to ministry gifts. Ministry is trusting the One we have come to know. Trusting the One who invades the impossible with the supernatural. God did not put His Spirit in us to *do* church and conduct meetings. The Spirit comes to reveal the Father and Son to us. From this knowledge we bring His love and power to the world. The focus is to be on His presence, recognising that the presents will follow.

Placing a high value on His presence results in looking to build a personal life and congregational life that provides a place of habitation for God, not simply visitation. The Lord is attracted to love, intimacy, friendship and unity. His Word continually lifts up these characteristics through the Old and New Testaments as attracting blessing and being His highest concern. As we achieve greater depths of love, intimacy, friendship and unity, the Lord's presence will come in greater and greater measures. While we are to earnestly desire spiritual gifts (1 Corinthians 14:1) and we are to put on love as the overriding prerequisite for the expression of the gifts (1 Corinthians 13:1-3, 13).

When we pursue presents before presence, we build atmospheres and anointings where the encounters with the Lord are encouraging but are self oriented. We need to cultivate an appetite for God where the anointing draws people to a lifestyle of seeking God, accompanied by empowerment and equipping from Heaven so that others can be touched by God through us.

Jesus himself is the pearl of great price (Matthew 13:45-46). We diminish His value when we seek the gifts more than the gift-giver. Times of refreshing come in the presence of the Lord (Acts 3:19). It is out of these times that His life flows. The gifts are simply the vehicle. Compassion and mercy are the fuel. When we are in His presence we receive His heart. His heart is for the tormented, afflicted and infirm. Jesus was always prepared to give the Father's presents to others but He came for the sake of relationship with God above everything else.

MYSTERY BEFORE MASTERY
BUT NOT WITHOUT MASTERY

Albert Einstein, a man who mastered so much in understanding maths and physics said, "The most beautiful thing we can experience is the mysterious" and "Imagination is more important than knowledge." William Blake said, "The imagination is evidence of the Divine." Henry Miller added, "Until we accept the fact that life itself is founded in mystery, we shall learn nothing."

Mystery is at the heart of a dynamic, growing relationship with God. Proverbs 25:2 asserts: *It is the glory of God to conceal a matter, but the glory of kings is to search out a matter.*

In general, Western Christians have been raised to rely on and believe in logic. We have been taught to think in categories and in a neat linear fashion. We prefer to work with known principles and anything unknown is seen to be wrong or possibly dangerous. Consequently, our preference is to master life. Mastery is also a way of controlling the way life unfolds.

Mastery seeks satisfaction as its goal. It seeks to be safe, certain and comfortable believing that this is the pinnacle of life. In fact, it is the place of death. Satisfaction leads to complacency. We stop crying out, contending for and pursuing more. Dissatisfaction, handled properly, is a gift because it embraces mystery and our need for God to show us more and do more. The Creator wants to create and He wants to share the joy of the process with us.

> **DISSATISFACTION IS A GIFT BECAUSE IT EMBRACES MYSTERY AND OUR NEED FOR GOD TO SHOW US MORE AND DO MORE.**

God hides things *for* us not *from* us. Like all parents, He delights in a child's search for what is hidden. He makes it challenging to find but rejoices in the child's delight of having found what was hidden. This is the thrill of an Easter egg hunt for both child and adult.

When we place mastery before mystery we are going to be discouraged and disappointed. All too often we have inaccurate time frames that surround our expectations of when we will arrive or when something will happen. We over project and under perform not realising that the Lord wants us to enjoy the adventure with all its risks and uncertainties. When mastery is first, we often abort the process that God begun in us. Similar to the formation of stalactites and stalagmites, we need to trust the slow and random drip until one day we have the 'ah ha' experience.

A performance based mind-set will drive towards mastery. The fear and insecurity of performance seeks resolution and takes too much responsibility for the outcome. Mastery becomes a matter of personal pride, meeting needs for security and safety that the Lord wants to change in us. An acceptance based mind-set implicitly believes in the goodness of God while knowing there is permission to seek God for the answer to the mystery. Finally, we also need to keep in mind that there are some things that we will never understand because we are the creation, not the Creator.

NAMING BEFORE NUMBERING
BUT NOT WITHOUT NUMBERING

Names and numbers are both features of the Biblical record. The Lord clearly has an interest in both. Our interaction with both is necessary and helpful. However, the priority we place upon them will impact whether we move further into our voyage of mercy.

The Lord wants us to participate in the power and influence of naming. As part of creation, *God formed every beast of the field and every bird of the sky, and brought them to the man to see what HE WOULD CALL THEM; and whatever the man called a living creature, that was its name (Genesis 2:19. Capitals my emphasis). In fact, Adam was on a roll when God brought his help mate to him Adam said, This is now bone of my bones, and flesh of my flesh, SHE SHALL BE CALLED WOMAN, because she was taken out of Man* (Genesis 2:23. Capitals my emphasis).

When it comes to names there can often be a clear *because*. For example, Eve's name, woman was because she was taken out of man. The naming of people and places in the Bible is often for a reason and purpose. Preachers see lessons in the way names in the Bible can be instructive. Kris Vallotton, in his description of Nehemiah's confrontation with his enemies, provides one of any number of examples of this when he writes: *'ONO' means 'strength' and it represent the place of the enemy's strength. It is important for us not to fall for the tactics of the enemy by going down to the valley of his strength. If you venture down there, you will discover why the place is called 'Oh No!'.*[4]

Numbers also have a significant part to play in the Biblical narrative. An entire book of the Old Testament is devoted to them. Numbers are clearly and precisely stated in a wide range of places where money and material wealth are brought in offerings, where sacrifices are being made on special occasions, when the construction of something is being described, when armies are being assembled and arrayed against one another. Again, they are used by preachers to inspire faith and action for the purposes of God. The New Testament has numbers in the context of miracles and the growth of the early church.

The Lord changes people's names throughout the Bible. Jacob to Israel, Simon to Peter, and Saul to Paul are some of the more notable ones. These name changes are always for a purpose. Buried in that purpose is an increase in influence for the sake of God's purposes on the earth. The increase in influence also affects the *numbers* that are recorded around that person's life story.

The most instructive of these name changes and its relation to numbers is in Abram's life. Let's pick up the dialogue in Genesis 17:3,

Abram fell on his face, and God talked with him, saying, "As for Me, behold My covenant is with you, And you will be the father of a multitude of nations. No longer shall your name be called Abram, But your name shall be Abraham for I will make you the father of a multitude of nations."

Abram means exalted father. Abraham means father of a multitude. The name change both represented, and preceded, a change in the numbers that were to accompany his life's story and his ancestry.

Within the broader discussion of acceptance and performance, I believe this is a very salient and relevant thought. Is it possible that the church has unwittingly borrowed or bought into the standards and culture of the world? Has the church placed performance before acceptance in deeming it necessary and acceptable to use church size as indicators of success and importance? Have we lost sight of the fact that our name, our identity in Christ, is more important than our numbers? We are Christians, that is, followers of the Christ, the chosen one of God, the Alpha and Omega, the One to whom all authority has been given. Maybe if Paul was writing to the Western church today he might say:

So then, let no one boast in NUMBERS. For all things belong to you, whether the size of your church, or bank balance, or car or the world or life or death or things present or things to come; all thing belong to you, and you belong to Christ; and Christ belongs to God (My adaptation of 1 Corinthians 3:21-23).

Now we all know that we are not to boast in numbers. I choose to believe that those who hold numbers up do so for a variety of well intentioned purposes. For example, to glorify God, to inspire faith, to inspire action, to facilitate breakthrough to name a few.

...THOSE WITH PERFORMANCE BASED MIND-SETS ARE TORMENTED BY THIS USE OF NUMBERS.

However, those with performance based mind-sets are tormented by this use of numbers. These mind-sets and the evil one, distort the message and deceive people into comparison and self worth based on performance.

When numbering comes before naming many people lose sight of who and whose they are, and sometimes forget altogether. They are ensnared and fall back into self-effort. If I just go to this conference, get this person to pray for me, work harder, do this course, implement this strategy, pray and fast more, then God will add more. However, when naming comes before numbering, but not denying that numbers and measuring have their place, then it is not about what I do but what He has done, is doing, and will do with me. Is it possible that much of the stress, strain, striving and frantic activity of the Western church is influenced by an emphasis on numbers that is not helpful in the context of a performance based culture? Maybe the high burn out rate within the ranks of church leadership is because the numbers game is being used to trap these fine men and women onto a battleground where their secret inner kingdom is not capable of winning the battle.

I certainly know for myself that, like the Australian cricketer in the TV commercial, it was true that, "Numbers, they haunt me and define me". Now I am free I find it difficult to recognise the person I was only twelve months ago.

CHARASMATIC EXPERIENCE BEFORE SPIRITUAL DISCIPLINES BUT NOT WITHOUT SPIRITUAL DISCIPLINES

My story and insights are nearing their end as I cycle back to where I began. In my opening comments I observed, "My thought was that there had to be more. More than I was experiencing. More of God to experience for those I was leading." I have always been a self disciplined person. Maintaining a consistent life of prayer and Bible study has not been difficult. In truth this is probably a by-product of my performance based approach to life, not some virtuous dimension of my character. Other spiritual disciplines such as fasting and solitude have always been present and I have a deep joy in corporate worship and fellowship. Yet, in and of themselves, these disciplines had not delivered me from the fear and insecurity generated by the way I responded to a performance based culture.

Mark Stibbe was again helpful in understanding why and how this could be the case. He writes:

As I have constantly shown, it is Jesus who has opened up the way by which slaves become sons. But Paul also says that it is the Holy Spirit who applies the benefits of the finished work of Christ to our lives...Without the empowering presence of the Holy Spirit, we cannot actually experience the glorious freedom of the children of God. We may know our freedom as an intellectual fact, but we will not know it as a heartfelt reality. There is therefore an unavoidable, charismatic dimension to our adoption.

During church history there has often been a neglect of the experience of the Holy Spirit. Frankly, it is amazing how quickly Paul's emphasis on 'demonstrations of the Spirit's power' fades from view...The means of getting from slavery to sonship undergoes a subtle change in the post-apostolic church. No longer is it the invasion of the fire of love that constitutes the key factor in the process. Now it is strenuous self-effort that gets a person from servile fear to filial love.[5]

My salvation experience was profoundly supernatural. Three days after accepting Jesus as my Lord and Saviour I was baptised in the Holy Spirit as evidenced by speaking in tongues. This happened when I was on my own, having no knowledge of this experience, let alone desire for it. I simply knew I loved Jesus

> **OUR HEART WILL ALWAYS TAKE US TO PLACES THAT OUR HEAD CANNOT REACH.**

and was asking for more. Charismatic experience came before spiritual disciplines but charismatic experience alone does not build a fruitful Christian life. Spiritual disciplines are necessary for spiritual growth but there are some things that require more. Our heart will always take us to places that our head cannot reach.

When we place spiritual disciplines before charismatic experience we generally think the Christian life is based in what we do more than what God does. We are invited to taste and see that the Lord is good (Psalm 34:8). Jesus provided many people with extraordinary experiences before they followed Him. Jesus pours revelations into our hearts that set us free.

Spiritual disciplines can position us for life changing encounters with God. However, it is the encounter that establishes and builds our relationship.

Last Thoughts

Somewhere along the way in my voyage of mercy I got bewitched. I can now see the access point for my deception was the unresolved fear and insecurity of my response to a performance based culture. The events from November 2004 to June 2005 unfolded at the leading of the Spirit. I then had another profound charismatic experience with some good friends, Hamish and Diane Divett in New Zealand. It was this experience that saw enough light from Heaven come into the darkness that allowed me to see with the greatest clarity that God accepted me.

After much consideration I have decided not to detail my experience in New Zealand. I cannot find the words to adequately convey the wonder of what took place in such a short period of time. It would focus too much attention on the event when it was really the process over the previous nine months that created the context for the event. In describing the experience I would need to explain the methodology the Divetts used called Refocussing©. I feel inadequate to do this and would not do it justice and would recommend readers visit the Refocussing website[6].

In general people are not wicked, they are weak. We all have unmet needs. These unmet needs, combined with the fact that we tend to see God as we are, not as He is, results in illusions about God. It is in these unmet needs and illusions that the devil makes his playground. He will do all he can to deceive us so that we don't rely on the Lord and

IN GENERAL PEOPLE ARE NOT WICKED, THEY ARE WEAK.

allow Him to be the greatest Father. On the other hand, Jesus stands in the midst of our daily life and cries out: *If anyone is thirsty, let him come to Me and drink* (John 7:37). When we are weak we thirst for help and answers. Jesus is the drink for the dry and thirsty places of our innermost world, our inner secret kingdom. Jesus has rivers of living water (John 7:38) that will heal and restore our brokenness. Jesus has forgiven what is wrong in our lives. Now He looks to bring a gift to minister to what is missing. In my case I was missing the assurance of my acceptance and the fullness of the Spirit of adoption.

Here ends the account of my journey so far. If anything I've written resonates with you, I encourage you to invite the Holy Spirit in to your own voyage of mercy. He will deal with the right issues in the right way at the right time. My simple intent was to describe the miracle that has set another part of me free. There are no prescriptive formulas. However, there is a very good God in Heaven who, as our Father, loves to bring pleasure to His children.

MATTERS DESERVING CONSIDERATION

Great improvisers are like priests, they are thinking only of their God.

STEPHANE GRAPPELLI

It appears to me that in the Australian church there may be an impending crisis for church leaders. As I move around and hear the struggles of other church leaders, I realize I am not alone in my struggle with the fear that is created and established through inappropriate responses to a performance based culture. I do not want to project my own experience onto others, but I am concerned.

Church leaders are one of the greatest resources of our community. The local church is the hope of the world. Across every segment of society there is a need for more good leaders not fewer. The church needs to do all it can to both nurture and support her leaders while effectively joining in the battle they face.

In this context, I have a number of, *What if...* scenarios that deserve consideration. I want to raise these issues and resist the temptation to prescribe the answers. Each theological and denominational

...IF THE STATUS QUO CONTINUES, I BELIEVE THAT MANY LEADERS ARE GOING TO BURN OUT OR DETONATE.

environment will offer its own unique set of boundaries that will affect the answers to my questions. However, if the status quo continues, I believe that many leaders are going to burn out or detonate.

Here are the insights of Keith Farmer on this matter. Keith has been in full time ministry for 40 years. He has trained thousands of people for ministry. He is now a spiritual coach for over 40 senior ministers, including me, around Australia.

For most of the last quarter of a century I have been involved in Theological Education and along with a team of colleagues came to believe that the essence of Christian discipleship which matures to be the basis of Christian leadership is Spiritual formation. From both a Biblical and practical perspective it seemed to us that training should be the integration of multiple emphases e.g. Biblical understanding and knowledge, practical skills and experience, community experience and accountability. However, without the growing capacity to love God with all of our heart, soul and strength and to love our neighbour as ourselves (Mark 12: 30-31a), the ministry leadership capacity would be at best severely restricted and more than likely prove to be too difficult at some stage.

In this manuscript Peter is seeking to put the spiritual formation emphasis at the centre of all discipleship and ministry.

My very recent ministry experience has majored on mentoring missional leaders. I am privileged to fulfil that role for a range of Australian Christian leaders and developing leaders. I have rapidly become quite aware that the key issues for which present missional leaders are looking and needing support centre on who they are in their roles. Spiritual, relational and emotional health issues are pivotal to them being able to continue to perform in their ministries. Performance and competitiveness pressures are increasing and even people who have experienced considerable success in the past are finding their leadership roles more and more difficult. The consumerist nature of Western Christianity whereby the church or ministry with the best and most gifted resources will attract the largest crowd is eating away at the motivation and is discouraging extremely committed, gifted people - Peter's thrust rightly affords achievement and performance an important place. However unless being secure in the love and grace of God is the key motivation, performance will at some stage falter.

The heart of the material presented seems to me to be in the chapter Before but not without. The concept that without the most important being in place as such nothing else really matters, is presented by Paul in 1 Corinthians 13: 1-3 with respect to the foundational place of love. As Peter very clearly expresses, this does not mean that other teachings are unimportant, but that if they take the primary place nothing of lasting value will be achieved.

.

There is nothing more important to Christian discipleship and long term transformational and missional leadership than the issues addressed so vulnerably, courageously, thoughtfully and persistently in these pages. Not only does the heart of what is expressed here reflect the heart of the gospel, it has the capacity to give a challenge to and even be a model for a truly authentic Christian leadership emphasis. This could revive our churches through deep revitalization of discipleship and therefore leadership.

When church growth is elevated above the spiritual health and well being of its leaders the church loses its prophetic edge. The Lord's primary agenda is our spiritual formation. He seeks our intimacy above our effort. He longs for our friendship above our service. He desires to release revelation to us where we desire that He brings us success. We are called by God to look to the unseen world but we want to emphasize the seen world. The conversation of church leaders' inevitability drifts back to key performance indicators and these fill their consciousness. What drops out of our conversation, drops out of our consciousness. When leaders are not discussing the life and work of God in their inner secret kingdom it takes on a place of lesser importance.

WHAT IF... THERE IS A PROBLEM?

"Woe to the rebellious children", declares the Lord, "Who execute a plan, but not Mine. And make an alliance, but not of My Spirit, in order to add sin to sin;" (Isaiah 30:1)

What if we have made an alliance with the performance base of our culture in the way we are 'doing church'? What if we are executing good plans before we are hearing the Lord's direction? What if the church has lost its prophetic nature by adopting standards of the world system it is in? Why, if as all the research shows, are people disinterested in the institutional church but very interested in Jesus? While all the teaching on leadership, systems, processes, structure, and techniques is necessary and helpful, has it in fact been overemphasized to the detriment of church spirituality?

Leaders are under pressure to perform. They find themselves fighting a rear guard action in dwindling and dying congregations; or they are trying to keep up with the bright and shining stars of growing mega churches; or they are leading a larger church and pursuing further growth. Whatever scenario they face, all have a genuine, heartfelt desire to advance the

THE REAL ISSUE COMES FROM THE INTERACTION BETWEEN A LEADER'S INNER SECRET KINGDOM AND THE NEED FOR GROWTH.

kingdom. The real issue comes from the interaction between a leader's inner secret kingdom and the need for growth.

Is it possible that leaders are presenting a superficial acceptance of the pursuit of growth, while in reality they are overwhelmed and trying to make it happen through self effort and the 'latest thing' that is working? If so, why would they do this? Also, if so, what impact is it having on their relationship with God?

How do congregations and denominations create safe places for their leaders to be real? Places to be open, transparent and vulnerable about the struggles of their inner secret kingdom? Places of refuge where permission is given to both acknowledge and face fear without being thought less of, patronized, rejected, punished or abandoned. Rather, they will experience the acceptance, affirmation and genuine support that allows the necessary space and time for the word of God to bring release, healing and freedom.

Is the spiritual life of a leader being inadvertently sacrificed on the altar of church growth? Is an emphasis on church growth, tapping into the fears created and established in the heart of a leader through their response to a performance based culture? If so, what needs to be done to help leaders to unravel the internal pressures?

WHAT IF... VULNERABILITY IS REQUIRED?

In Australia, Beyond Blue, is a secular initiative to take the stigma out of being depressed. It is both an awareness raising and education based approach to normalize the place of depression in our society. It promotes understanding and acceptance that depressed people should not be marginalised, rejected and seen as inadequate or hopeless. Rather, depression is a life issue that can afflict the best of us, for no apparent reason, and at any given time in our lives. Such normalization promotes a climate where being vulnerable and seeking help is seen as a good thing.

SUCH NORMALIZATION PROMOTES A CLIMATE WHERE BEING VULNERABLE AND SEEKING HELP IS SEEN AS A GOOD THING.

The same can be said of similar campaigns aimed at physical ailments such as breast cancer for women and prostate cancer for men. Where once people were embarrassed or fearful to seek help, it is now acceptable to talk about these issues. As a society we are now prepared to give those struggling with these diseases the time and space from their normal life duties to sort through the issues. We send a clear message of value and concern that everything will be done to ensure their well being is of the highest priority.

What if there is a need to acknowledge the place of fear inside church leaders and the need for them to be set free? Could we accept weakness and failure by normalizing it to the point where preventative help is sought rather than cleaning up the mess? How do we create cultures where leaders are sure that mercy will triumph over judgment? What if we need to honour vulnerability rather than reinforcing the perception that it is safer to wear a mask of competence and coping?

What if...Church Culture is Addictive and Co-dependent?

The literature on why people become addicted and also co-dependent highlights the place of acceptance and performance issues. Addictive and co-dependent behaviour patterns draw on unresolved issues of acceptance and performance.

Addictions can be used to mask and manage fears. Fear is an acronym for false expectations appearing real. When fear is at work a person will invariably make things matter in such a way that they feel inadequate or out of control. From God's perspective, some of the things our fears convince us are important, are wrong. We become captive to lies that we believe are truth. For example, to fail is bad and leads to rejection – "No it's not, it's normal and I can learn from it". However, if we believe it is bad, we develop behaviour that avoids failure or masks it. When church leaders are intimidated by failure they can become addicted to many things. It might be the pursuit of

WHEN CHURCH LEADERS ARE INTIMIDATED BY FAILURE THEY CAN BECOME ADDICTED TO MANY THINGS.

success, pornography or any number of other destructive behaviours that create the illusion of acceptance and performance.

What if church growth is overemphasised to the point where leaders are addicted to behaviour that could destroy them? How do we help church leaders find acceptance in God, not in their performance, either imagined or real, or success and the adrenalin it offers?

Co-dependence is an issue of unconsciously relying on relationships with others to feel good about ourselves. For a church leader it can be: "When I help you I feel good; when I can't help you I feel bad; therefore, I will pour my life out for you because I fear rejection, failure, being misunderstood." If boards, leadership teams or congregations are demanding, then a leader, may through co-dependence, expend their energy negatively to find acceptance. Such depletion of emotional and spiritual resources will result in a leader making errors of judgment that are damaging and dispiriting. Church life can be focused on the management of dysfunctional relationships and the advancement of God's kingdom becomes secondary.

What if an emphasis on performance before acceptance is creating co-dependent cultures? How do we build communities that have acceptance before performance but not without performance?

WHAT IF... LOVE IS THE KEY?

There is no fear in love; but perfect love casts out fear, because fear involves punishment, and the one who fears is not perfected in love (1 John 4:18).

What if love really is the highest of all Christian values? If fear is created through our response to a performance based culture how do we build communities that emphasize love? What would such expressions of love look like in the way we allow leaders to live their lives?

When we allow cultures where fear has to be managed and contained we are assigning people to captivity. As long as there is a perceived emphasis on performance we are potentially creating a culture that reflects this world. Fear assumes punishment and will result in people being closed down and isolated. Such a person is a prime target for demonic attack and influence. Yet Scripture is clear that love is key.

> **WHEN WE ALLOW CULTURES WHERE FEAR HAS TO MANAGED AND CONTAINED WE ARE ASSIGNING PEOPLE TO CAPTIVITY.**

What if we could help church leaders live in the confidence of being loved and accepted by God before they had to perform? At this point Graham Cooke's insights may be helpful:

In our thinking we must focus on mercy and grace or we will be mentally judging others. Jesus is 'with us' and He is 'for people'. Pharisees define themselves by what they are against, thus putting themselves on the wrong side of God. Jesus' appeal to the church is to 'be merciful just as your Father is merciful' (Luke 6:36). We are in a prophetic season of grace, so let's be gracious. It is God's kindness and goodness that lead people to repentance, not our hammer of revelation. God's love is impossible to resist. To communicate it properly, our hearts have to be soaked in that love. We need to be completely overwhelmed by the grace of God.[1]

Knowing God loves us, and experiencing it in the reality of our fellowship, creates a culture where love is valued as the key.

It is my hope and prayer that the matters raised in this final chapter provoke thought, consideration, discussion and action. I know good leaders who suffer from panic attacks, wrestle with pornography, live in a world of personal doubt, feel isolated and marginalised in their denomination, experience tension and strife in their own congregations, and mouth commitment to their current place of service, but in their hearts long for something different. How we love and support these men and women is critical.

APPENDICES

APPENDIX 1

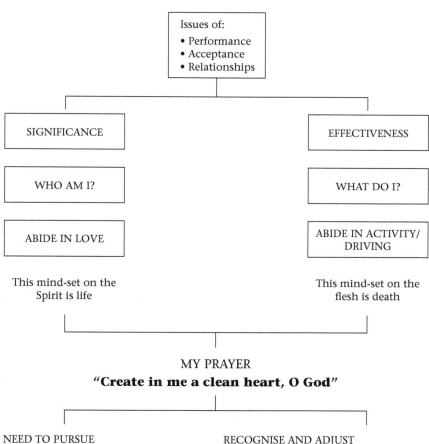

Issues of:
- Performance
- Acceptance
- Relationships

SIGNIFICANCE	EFFECTIVENESS
WHO AM I?	WHAT DO I?
ABIDE IN LOVE	ABIDE IN ACTIVITY/ DRIVING

This mind-set on the
Spirit is life

This mind-set on the
flesh is death

MY PRAYER
"Create in me a clean heart, O God"

NEED TO PURSUE

1. Giving up control of the things that matter most to me
2. Place my confidence in someone I cannot manage
3. Stop protecting myself
4. Be utterly dependent on God's willingness to give Himself to me
5. Live from resurrection power not emotional, mental, will power

RECOGNISE AND ADJUST

1. Effectiveness/fruitfulness comes from abiding in love/Jesus
2. Ministry and relationships can be controlled and contrived
3. Continual low grade fear
4. I'm tired of running the organization
5. What impact I am having on the life of the church

Appendix 2

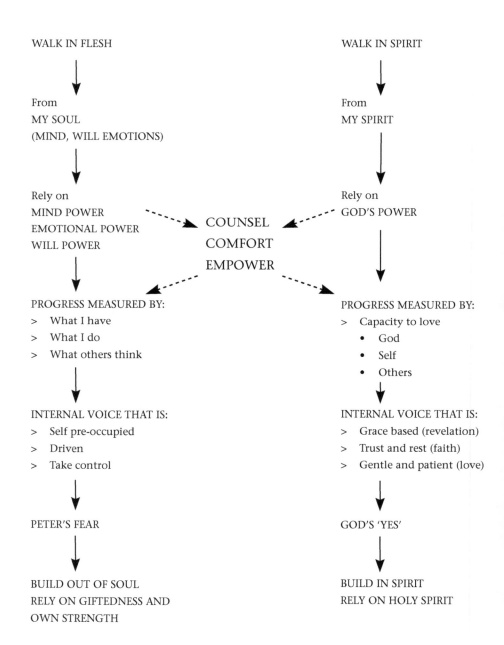

WALK IN FLESH

↓

From
MY SOUL
(MIND, WILL EMOTIONS)

↓

Rely on
MIND POWER
EMOTIONAL POWER
WILL POWER

COUNSEL
COMFORT
EMPOWER

↓

PROGRESS MEASURED BY:
> What I have
> What I do
> What others think

↓

INTERNAL VOICE THAT IS:
> Self pre-occupied
> Driven
> Take control

↓

PETER'S FEAR

↓

BUILD OUT OF SOUL
RELY ON GIFTEDNESS AND
OWN STRENGTH

WALK IN SPIRIT

↓

From
MY SPIRIT

↓

Rely on
GOD'S POWER

↓

PROGRESS MEASURED BY:
> Capacity to love
  • God
  • Self
  • Others

↓

INTERNAL VOICE THAT IS:
> Grace based (revelation)
> Trust and rest (faith)
> Gentle and patient (love)

↓

GOD'S 'YES'

↓

BUILD IN SPIRIT
RELY ON HOLY SPIRIT

NOTES

Chapter 3

1. Don Williams, *Jesus and Addiction*, (San Diego: Recovery Publishers, 1993), 1.

2. Ibid., 44

3. Ibid., 38 – 39

4. It is not my intention nor do I believe my mandate to cover this significant and important truth of grace. There are many wonderful books already dedicated to and available on this topic.

5. Bill Johnson & Kris Vallotton, *The Supernatural Ways of Royalty*, (Shippensburg: Destiny Image Publishers, 2006), 22.

Chapter 4

1. Bill Johnson & Kris Vallotton, *The Supernatural Ways of Royalty*, (Shippensburg : Destiny Image Publishers 2006)

2. Graham Cook, Being with God: Living in Dependence and Wonder, (Kent: Sovereign World. 2004)

3. Graham minsters in our church every year now. I have read his books, sat under his teaching and we have hung out together as friends. His ideas will be evident in my writing but I will not be able to accurately source them because they have become part of me. (The same could be said of Bill Johnson, Kris Vallotton, Phil Pringle, Fergus McIntyre, Hamish and Dianne Divett. Please forgive me if I do no ascribe the greatness of a thought to you when it was yours first.)

4. Just as with the topic of grace it is not my intention, nor do I believe my mandate to cover the significance and importance of the topic of the *Father Heart of God*. There are many wonderful books already dedicated to and available on this topic.

5. Johnson & Vallotton, *The Supernatural Ways of Royalty*, 52.

6. This statement I first heard on a preaching C.D. with Michael Pitts speaking

7. These ideas have been birthed in me through Bill Johnson. Bill preaches in our church. He is a friend. Two of his books contain these ideas: a) Bill Johnson, *When Heaven Invades Earth. A practical guide to a life of miracles,* (Shippensburg: Destiny Image Publishers, 2004).

b) Bill Johnson, *The Supernatural Power of a Transformed Mind. Access to a life of miracles,* (Shippensburg: Destiny Image Publishers, 2005).

8. A thought for those who preach and teach: you can only impart what you are Therefore, become something before you speak about it. Do not study to speak. Study to be changed and communicate out of the change.

Chapter 5

1. Mark Stibbe, *From Orphans to Heirs: Celebrating our Spiritual Adoption*, (Oxford: The Bible Reading Fellowship, 2005).

2. Ibid., 115-118

3. Ibid., 118

4. Ibid., 126

Chapter 6

1. Janet Hagberg & Robert Guelich, *The Critical Journey: Stages in the Life of Faith*, (Salem: Sheffield Publishing Company, 2005)

2. Ibid., 123

3. Ibid., 121

4. Ibid

5. Ibid., 232-25

Chapter 7

1. Bill Johnson, *The Supernatural Power of a Transformed Mind. Access to a life of miracles,* (Shippensburg: Destiny Image Publishers, 2005).

Chapter 8

1. CS Lewis, First and Second Things. An essay from God in the Dock. Essays on Theology and Ethics (Grand Rapids: Eerdmans, Reprinted 1994, Walter Hooper editor)

2. Kris Vallotton, *Present and Vertical Truth* – A New Operating System, Teaching Notes, School of Supernatural Ministry, Bethel Church 933 College View Drive - Redding, CA 96003 www.ibethel.org

3. Johnson & Vallotton, *The Supernatural Ways of Royalty*, 91.

4. Ibid., 111

5. Mark Stibe, *From Orphans to Heirs: Celebrating our Spiritual Adoption,* (Oxford: The Bible Reading Fellowship, 2005), 137 – 138

6. Refocussing© web address: www.refocussing.com

Chapter 9

1. Graham Cooke, *Approaching the Heart of Prophecy: A Journey into Encouragement, Blessing and Prophetic Gifting,* (Winston-Salem: Punch Press, 2006), 23 – 26.

CPSIA information can be obtained
at www.ICGtesting.com
Printed in the USA
BVHW060805260122
627130BV00015B/1317